Editors' Preface to Macmillan Studies in Economics

The rapid growth of academic literature in the field of economics has posed serious problems for both students and teachers of the subject. The latter find it difficult to keep pace with more than a few areas of the subject so that an inevitable trend towards specialism emerges. The student quickly loses perspective as the maze of theories and models grows, particularly at a time when so much reappraisal of the established paradigms is taking place.

The aim of the 'Macmillan Studies in Economics' is to offer students, and perhaps some teachers as well, short, reasonably critical overviews of developments in selected areas of economics, particularly those in which current controversies are to be found. As far as possible the titles have been selected to form an integrated whole, although inevitably entire areas have been neglected as being unsuited to the style, format and length of the titles in the series.

In some cases the volumes are rather more like essays than surveys. In most cases, however, the aim is to survey the salient literature in a critical fashion. The level of understanding required to read the volumes varies with the complexity of the subject, but they have been generally written to suit the second- and third-year undergraduate seeking to place his reading of the detailed literature in an over-all context. They are *not* textbooks. Instead they seek to give the kind of perspective that might well be lost by reading longer textbooks on their own, or by reading articles in journals. In particular, they should be most suited to pre-examination revision periods. They are not intended to substitute for the essential reading and assimilation of the original works that they seek to survey and assess.

MACMILLAN STUDIES IN ECONOMICS

General Editors: D. C. ROWAN and G. R. FISHER

Executive Editor: D. W. PEARCE

Published
R. W. Anderson: THE ECONOMICS OF CRIME
John Burton: WAGE INFLATION
Susan Charles: HOUSING ECONOMICS
Ben Fine: MARX'S 'CAPITAL'
Douglas Fisher: MONETARY POLICY
Miles Fleming: MONETARY THEORY
C. J. Hawkins and D. W. Pearce: CAPITAL INVESTMENT APPRAISAL
C. J. Hawkins: THEORY OF THE FIRM
David F. Heathfield: PRODUCTION FUNCTIONS
Dudley Jackson: POVERTY
P. N. Junankar: INVESTMENT: THEORIES AND EVIDENCE
J. F. King: LABOUR ECONOMICS
John King and Philip Regan: RELATIVE INCOME SHARES
J. A. Kregel: THE THEORY OF ECONOMIC GROWTH
J. A. Kregel: THEORY OF CAPITAL
Richard Lecomber: ECONOMIC GROWTH VERSUS THE ENVIRONMENT
George McKenzie: THE MONETARY THEORY OF INTERNATIONAL TRADE
David J. Mayston: THE IDEA OF SOCIAL CHOICE
C. A. Nash: PUBLIC VERSUS PRIVATE TRANSPORT
S. K. Nath: A PERSPECTIVE OF WELFARE ECONOMICS
Anthony Peaker: ECONOMIC GROWTH IN MODERN BRITAIN
D. W. Pearce: COST-BENEFIT ANALYSIS
Maurice Peston: PUBLIC GOODS AND THE PUBLIC SECTOR
Nicholas Rau: TRADE CYCLES: THEORY AND EVIDENCE
David Robertson: INTERNATIONAL TRADE POLICY
Charles K. Rowley: ANTITRUST AND ECONOMIC EFFICIENCY
C. H. Sharp: TRANSPORT ECONOMICS
G. K. Shaw: FISCAL POLICY
R. Shone: THE PURE THEORY OF INTERNATIONAL TRADE
M. J. Stabler: AGRICULTURAL ECONOMICS AND RURAL LAND-USE
Frank J. B. Stilwell: REGIONAL ECONOMIC POLICY
A. P. Thirlwall: FINANCING ECONOMIC DEVELOPMENT
R. Kerry Turner and Clive Collis: THE ECONOMICS OF PLANNING
John Vaizey: THE ECONOMICS OF EDUCATION
J. van Doorn: DISEQUILIBRIUM ECONOMICS
Peter A. Victor: ECONOMICS OF POLLUTION
Graham Walshe: INTERNATIONAL MONETARY REFORM
Michael G. Webb: PRICING POLICIES FOR PUBLIC ENTERPRISES
E. Roy Weintraub: CONFLICT AND CO-OPERATION IN ECONOMICS
E. Roy Weintraub: GENERAL EQUILIBRIUM THEORY

Forthcoming
A. Ziderman: MANPOWER TRAINING: THEORY AND POLICY

Housing Economics

SUSAN CHARLES

Lecturer in Economics, University of Loughborough

First published 1977 by
THE MACMILLAN PRESS LTD
London and Basingstoke
Associated companies in Delhi Dublin
Hong Kong Johannesburg Lagos Melbourne
New York Singapore and Tokyo

Typeset in Baskerville by
PREFACE LTD
Salisbury, Wiltshire
Printed and bound in Great Britain by
UNWIN BROTHERS LTD
The Gresham Press, Old Woking, Surrey

British Library Cataloguing in Publication Data

Charles Susan
    Housing economics. — (Macmillan studies in
    economics).
    1. Housing
    I. Title   II. Series
    338.4'7'30154   HD7287

    ISBN 0—333—19827—1

Contents

1 Introduction 7
    Housing as a consumer durable 7
    Housing markets 8
    Some definitions 10
    State of the stock and government policy 11

2 The House Purchase Market 14
    The process of buying and selling houses 14
    Defining the market 16
    Determinants of demand 19
    Determinants of supply 23
    Price level 27
    Relative prices 28

3 Finance for House Purchase 33
    Sources of finance 33
    Building societies 38

4 New Building 44
    The building industry 44
    Costs of new housing 47
    Productivity and design 49
    Improving the housing stock 52

5 The Market for Rented Accommodation 55
    Determinants of demand 55
    Determinants of supply — private sector 58
    Determinants of supply — public sector 63
    Summary 70

    Bibliography 71

1 Introduction

HOUSING AS A CONSUMER DURABLE

Houses are assets which are demanded for the flow of services they produce over their lifetime. Thus, the starting point for an analysis of housing is the demand for housing services. These are bought either by buying the asset itself or by renting it. Therefore, the demand for houses to purchase and the demand for rented accommodation are derived demands. Housing gives a diverse bundle of services associated with shelter and comfort, independence and privacy, status and, like all durables, services of a security and investment nature. These services may be bought in various combinations. For example, investment characteristics exist in houses which are owned but not, to the occupier, in those which are rented. Further, each service may be purchased in varying quantities. For example, shelter services vary from the basic necessary for protection from the elements, to 'luxury' levels which include central heating, ample room space and the like. Ability to buy housing services in varying combinations and to various degrees implies that housing is a heterogeneous commodity.

The choice between renting and buying and between different types of house thus begins with the utility assigned to each housing service by households. These utility functions are converted into demand functions via economic variables of prices, income, wealth and suchlike. The formation of demand functions for buying and renting are discussed in Chapters 2 and 5, respectively. Little can be said here about the formation of utility functions, but three general points might serve to guide the reader.

First, owning, with its increased services of freedom, security and status, is typically regarded as preferable to renting. Second, although housing gives services which are necessary (for example, minimal shelter from the elements) most individuals consume housing in excess of this level (for example, more or less comfortable). Thus, at the level consumed, housing is not typically a necessity. Hence there is no *a priori* reason to expect housing demands to be particularly unresponsive to changes in economic variables. Third, preferences have changed over time, as innovations have occurred and standards of living improved. Houses are long-lived assets, and changing preferences may foreshorten their life or create a demand for their renovation.

HOUSING MARKETS

Ability to rent or buy creates two separate, though not independent, markets within housing (Figure 1.1). In the rented market, demand arises from households who opt to purchase their housing services by renting houses. Supply is through public and private bodies. Conceptual division of this market into public and private sectors is necessary because they are differently motivated. This is discussed in Chapter 5. In the house purchase market, demand arises from those households who wish to purchase their housing services by buying the asset (owner occupation), and landlords, both public and private, who wish to buy the asset in order to enter the rented market. There are two sources of supply. New accommodation is supplied by the building industry (which, incidentally, is also a supplier to other markets, as illustrated in Figure 1.1) but, since housing has a long life, there is also an extensive supply of secondhand dwellings. The house purchase market is discussed in Chapter 2 and the building industry is discussed in more depth in Chapter 4.

Because housing is an expensive asset, money is usually borrowed in order to purchase it. Thus, housing has a third market; that concerned with the finance of house purchase.

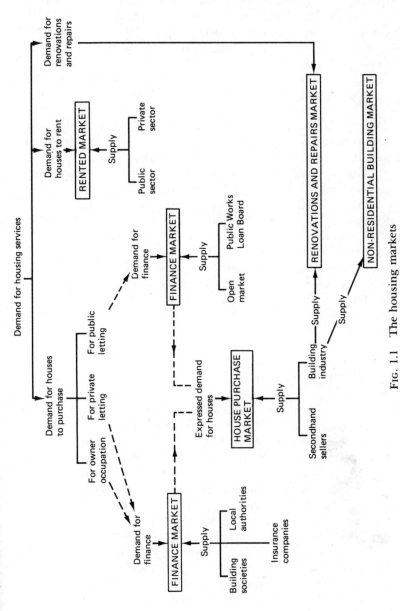

Fig. 1.1 The housing markets

9

In this book it has proved convenient to split the discussion of the finance market between Chapters 3 and 5. In Chapter 3 the finance of private purchase is considered, while Chapter 5 gives brief attention to the finance of public purchase.

There is one further market which may be added to this conceptualisation of the housing system; that concerned with renovations and repairs. This is a third derived demand from the demand for housing services, because renovation and repair to the asset is a way of improving or maintaining the flow of services it produces. Supply in this market is again from the building industry. This is discussed very briefly at the end of Chapter 4.

To this basic framework of housing as a group of linked markets, a further dimension may be added. Since housing is an immobile asset, demand in one locality cannot be met by the supply of a house in another. Thus, the housing systems must be conceived as a series of local ones. Since housing is a heterogeneous commodity, it is also necessary to envisage sub-markets within local markets, according to house characteristics. This concept is investigated at the end of Chapter 2.

SOME DEFINITIONS

Throughout this book, the terms 'house,' 'dwelling' and 'accommodation' are used interchangeably and should be taken to mean any separate unit of accommodation. The term 'household' is loosely defined as meaning one or more persons who share a common budget. The housing stock is the number of dwellings in existence at any point in time. This should be kept distinct from the flow of houses which constitute supply on to the purchase and renting markets. In this book, supply is taken to mean the flow of houses whose owners are currently looking for buyers or tenants. Once a house is bought or let, it ceases to be part of supply, but remains part of the stock. Thus, only a fraction of the stock is available for supply in any one period. The stock adjusts as new building occurs. Since new building is only about 2 per cent of the stock each year, adjustment is slow. Supply adjusts with the rate of new building and resale and is more flexible. Demand is, similarly, the flow of buyers and would-be tenants who are currently searching for houses. This concept should be kept distinct from the number of households, the stock counterpart to the housing stock. Once a household has found accommodation, it ceases to be part of demand.

Demand should also be distinguished from need. Need is a normative concept of a shortfall from some desired level of consumption of housing services. Unlike demand, it is not associated with willingness to pay on the part of the consumer. Thus, if there are more households than houses, and a societal goal is that every family should have a house, we may say that we need x more houses to remove the deficit. Whether or not x additional houses will be demanded, depends upon prices and individual willingness to pay.

STATE OF THE STOCK AND GOVERNMENT POLICY

In a book of this length it is inevitable that some things receive scant attention. In this case it was decided to concentrate on the positive analysis of the housing markets. This has meant that two areas are largely untouched: a description of the housing stock and its occupiers, and a normative analysis of policy. This section will make a few very general comments, but the reader is referred to the bibliography for more detail.

In 1974, the distribution of the U.K. housing stock over tenure types was 52 per cent owner-occupied, 31 per cent rented from the public sector and 17 per cent rented privately. This situation is the result of a century-long decline in private renting and a concomitant rise in the other two forms of tenure. Specific reasons for the decline in rented accommodation, which accounted for something like 90 per cent of the stock in 1914, are discussed in

11

Chapter 5. The distribution of households over tenure types is linked with income. Highest incomes are associated with owner occupation and lowest with private renting.

The stock of houses is now roughly in balance with the number of households, after long periods of shortages, particularly following the two world wars. However, it is unevenly distributed across the country, causing local scarcities. Further, some of the stock is deemed to be of unsatisfactory standard. The percentage of households living in accommodation which is substandard with regard to the old formal definition of the presence of basic amenities (hot water, bath and indoor toilet) is falling to single figures. However, definitions of what is satisfactory are subjective and have tended to rise with rising standards of living.

There is no overall government policy towards housing. Instead, there is a large number of unco-ordinated policies. Some are concerned with redressing specific malfunctions of the market; for example, government interest in building society behaviour (instability), the original rent control measures (short-run crisis shortages), aid towards housing associations (long-run decline of private renting) and action on land prices (inelastic supply). However, most policies have been concerned with the broader and vaguer problem of need. Housing is characterised as a special good (a merit good), one which society is concerned to see that its members consume sufficient of. Thus, the aim of policy is generally stated as being to ensure sufficient houses, at the right place and time and of the right type, for the population. Further, the houses must be of acceptable standard and within the financial means of the occupants. This goal creates needs to be met by policies which are difficult to estimate (what price is within the means of occupants?) and take no account of the opportunity cost of resources. Individual measures to remove need are not linked into an overall strategy. Instead, each deals with a specific aspect and tends to ignore the wider effects on the market and on other policies.

Measures to increase the housing stock have been restricted to subsidising the building of publicly owned

12

houses. Logical during times of overall shortages, this policy has become less useful now that shortages are local and for particular categories of households such as the mobile and the larger family. It is a very general stimulus to building. Measures to improve standards include policies of slum clearance and rehousing, overcrowding and overspill developments and renovation of older houses. These are problems which, by their nature, never end. Measures to control standards include building regulations and the implementation of Parker—Morris standards, which are standards for living and storage space developed for local authority housing in the Parker—Morris Report, *Homes for Today and Tomorrow* (H.M.S.O., 1961). Although logical in a narrow way, these policies often have undesirable side-effects. For example slum clearance and high building standards raise the cost of housing. Measures to reduce the cost of housing have been the most frequent actions. These include rent controls, subsidised council housing, rent rebates and allowances and tax relief on mortgage interest to the owner-occupier. Taken together, these policies are regressive, rather than linked to ability to pay. Further, they are questionable actions in times of long-run shortages. Consumption is stimulated, but the stock of housing is slow to respond, thus prices tend to rise.

In short, government interference is extensive but without a comprehensive strategy, or even any clear idea of what is wanted. The coming government study, *Review of Housing Finance*, might alter this, however. (This review, which should be published in 1977, is intended to take an overall view of government finance in all housing sectors.) Although these questions are large, we make no apology for ignoring them in this book. A prior knowledge of how the housing markets function is necessary to any successful policy.

2   The House Purchase Market

This chapter, in analysing the house purchase market, concentrates upon the demand and supply of houses for owner occupation, although much of what is said about the supply of new dwellings applies equally to the production of houses for the public market sector. The plan of the chapter is, first, to consider the process by which the owner-occupied market works, then the main determinants of demand and supply will be discussed and, finally, attention is paid to the determination of relative house prices.

THE PROCESS OF BUYING AND SELLING HOUSES

Participants in this market do not usually act unaided. The fact that a large amount of money is involved, that valuation of the good is made difficult by its variety and that individuals typically enter the market rarely and therefore have a poor knowledge of it, leads them to seek expert guidance. The main suppliers of such guidance are estate agents (in Scotland the estate agent is less prominent and his function is frequently performed by a solicitor), surveyors and solicitors. Estate agents provide information about the state of the market and act as a link through which buyer and seller may meet. The function of surveyors is to value property in terms of its physical condition and the state of the market. Their services are employed by the seller, through estate agents, and by the buyer, through building societies, or on his own volition. Solicitors are employed by both parties to handle the legal aspects of sale, search for ownership, drawing up of contracts and so on. To this list of bodies involved in the process of buying and selling, building societies might be added. These are not informational aids, but since most buyers use a mortgage loan from them to finance their purchase, they are involved. In order that their money is secure, building societies will assess both borrower and property before granting loans.

Such expert bodies serve the useful purpose of reducing the susceptibility of participants in the market to mistakes through ignorance. Their existence, however, has two other effects. First, they may influence both behaviour and prices. They are involved in price setting and thus their opinions are relevant as well as the actual state of the market. Further, they might bias behaviour; for example, building societies have been accused of being prejudiced against older property, and estate agents have been accused of being colour prejudiced (see [13] and [51], p. 145). As a result, a full understanding of the market may require analysis of their behaviour. With the exception of building society behaviour, this type of study is in its infancy and, regrettably, we must ignore these institutions. The second side-effect is to make transactions' costs high. The buyer must pay surveyor's and solicitor's fees and the seller must pay estate agent's and solicitor's fees (although in Northern Ireland the buyer, not the seller, pays the estate agent's fees). These costs are large and provide a disincentive to frequent movement, which implies slow personal adjustment to economic variables. For example, a household experiencing a steadily rising income will make only infrequent adjustments to housing consumption, in line with income, because of the high costs of moving.

Clearly, the process of buying and selling takes time. First, there is the time spent in searching for a house or a buyer. This is not costless and the cost will vary between individuals depending on their circumstances, in particular the urgency of completing a transaction. Hence, both participants must make a trade-off decision. The buyer must compare search costs with costs due to the risk of buying a house which is not the best bargain in the market, for bargain hunting takes time. The seller must make a similar decision, between selling quickly and selling at a

15

high price. Thus, individual decisions are made in the light of search costs as well as price; these costs should, therefore, be included in an analysis of the market. Again, the process through which they affect the market is not well understood, and we can do no more than mention them.

Once searching activities are over, a second time lapse occurs whilst negotiations take place. This is largely determined from the time it takes building societies and solicitors to perform their function. Throughout this period, the house is only sold subject to contract; either party can withdraw up until the time contracts are exchanged (an exception to this is in Scotland, where the bid is legally binding). There are thus risks of wasting time and money from stopping search activities and starting proceedings towards sale. One further complexity to the market may be added. Due to the prevalence of the secondhand market, many sellers are on both sides of the market at the same time. Most seek to co-ordinate the sale of their old house with the purchase of the new one. This increases the risks and time of the negotiation period; transactions are linked in a chain and any one hitch affects all.

Throughout this process, price is flexible. The seller's asking price may be varied during the search period and the agreed selling price is subject to bargaining during the negotiation period. For purposes of market analysis, interest is in the final, agreed price.

DEFINING THE MARKET

The market will be analysed by abstracting from the complexities discussed in the previous section and by considering the factors which determine demand and supply. Before commencing, it is necessary to define the concepts which will be used. First, the time period over which the model is concerned to describe behaviour must be specified. Briefly, there are three possibilities — a period short enough for there to be no change in the stock of houses only in its

16

ownership, a short-run period in which construction and demolition occurs, and a long-run period allowing sufficient time for the entire stock to adjust. For most purposes, it is the short-run period which is relevant. Thus, we will be concerned with the sale of new as well as second-hand houses. Since it takes time to build houses, short-run adjustments operate with a lag.

Second, the limits of the market must be made clear. A market is usually defined according to the closeness of substitutes, and the fact that houses are geographically fixed means that identical houses in different areas are not good substitutes. It is thus quite possible for a situation of excess demand to exist in one area alongside another in a state of excess supply. There might be some movement of population from high-priced excess demand areas to low-priced excess supply areas in response to price differentials, but this is not likely to be significant compared to the pull of employment opportunities. Adjustment will occur in the longer run as new construction is concentrated in excess demand areas and houses become obsolete and are not replaced in excess supply areas, but this may not be sufficient to allow the national market to be treated as a whole in the short run. For this reason, it is desirable to consider the local market rather than the national one.

Even within a locality, housing is a heterogeneous commodity. Consumers will regard houses as varying in value according to their external, locational setting and their internal or dwelling attributes of size, type and amenities. For example, few consumers would regard a four-bedroomed, detached house in a quiet, suburban area as a close substitute for a two-up-two-down terraced house next door to the railway station. It would be difficult to make further divisions into sub-markets according to housing attributes, but we must recognise that the market is far from homogeneous. Thus, for convenience, the general price level of housing for a local market is used here, but later consideration will be given to how relative prices are formulated.

This heterogeneity in housing presents measurement

problems. As for all durable goods, people desire houses for the flow of services they provide. Since this flow will vary with the attributes of each house, merely counting the number of houses demanded and supplied is a very poor measure. The quantity of housing services demanded, for instance, will determine the quantity *and* the quality of houses demanded. An ideal measure would be in terms of quality-adjusted units of housing. As will be illustrated later on in this section, this has been attempted in some studies. Where economists' ingenuity has failed them, and measurement is in terms of numbers only, we would expect the measured responsiveness of demand and supply to be less than the true one.

This brings us to our final definition, the concept of demand and supply. The discussion is in terms of market functions, ideally measured in quality-adjusted units. Further, they are flow concepts. Demand is to be understood as the flow of households who, in one unit of time, are looking for houses to purchase. Supply is the flow of houses which, during that time, are put up for sale. This formulation should be kept distinct from a second way of looking at the market; that of the stock adjustment model. This method uses the two stock variables, the number of houses and the number of households, as supply and demand respectively. It therefore concentrates upon adjustment of the housing stock towards equilibrium, rather than the more usual, but narrower, market adjustments in flows of buyers and sellers. (For a comparison of these two formulations, see [84], where they are set out side by side.) In this flow model, demand will consist of first-time buyers and existing house owners who wish to move within the owner-occupied tenure group. Supply will be the sum of newly built or converted houses and houses being resold as their owners move. It might be thought that, since existing owner-occupiers who move within this tenure group appear on both sides of the market, they can be ignored for the purposes of formulating the model. In some studies this has indeed been done, but it requires that houses be treated as homogeneous. For, if an existing owner-occupier is

18

moving to a better house, he is supplying less quality-adjusted units than he is demanding.

DETERMINANTS OF DEMAND

(a) *Demographic Factors* The most important demographic variable is the rate of household formation. This is closely associated with marriage, but not entirely. Newly married couples may remain with their parents for a while, and single people may set up home on their own. It is also not a truly independent variable, since the decision to create a household may be influenced by the cost of housing. Nevertheless, in general, it holds true that demand rises with the rate of household formation. Migration is a second factor which will influence a local market; this is frequently associated with employment opportunities. Demand will rise as immigration rises. Demand will also vary according to the distribution of families at different stages in their life-cycles. The size of a household will vary over its life and may be expected to cause demand as the household moves to adjust house size to family size. Again, this is not a truly independent variable. If the cost of housing is high, the expanding family might choose to double up rather than buy a bigger house.

(b) *Income* As income rises, demand will rise. This may be due to higher rates of household formation, movement from the rented sector to the owner-occupied sector (on the assumption that the latter is the preferred tenure to which individuals may be barred due to income) and movement by existing owner-occupiers to bigger and better houses, or even second homes. The concept of income which is relevant needs to be considered. First, since a household is interested in the spending power of its income, real income is more appropriate than money income. Further, since housing is a consumer durable which will provide a flow of services over a number of years, it is not current income which will be of concern, but permanent income. That is, any transitory component of current income will be ignored when deciding what house to purchase. For this reason, it has been argued that it is only the income of the head of the household which is relevant, since any children who are earning and contributing towards expenses currently cannot be expected to do so for long. Finally, buyers may be expected to consider net rather than gross pay. Since interest payments on mortgage loans are tax deductible, a rational buyer would be expected to take this into account. Thus, the relevant measure is net income allowing for relief on mortgage interest, i.e. net income after buying the house, not before.

As was stated previously, to use the number of houses demanded when measuring the income elasticity of demand is unsophisticated. It would give a low estimate of the responsiveness of demand, since it would hide any tendency for people to demand better houses as their incomes rise. Some reflection of quality-adjusted demand may be achieved by using a surrogate such as the rateable value of property demanded or by using expenditure on housing. If better housing costs more, a rise in income which leads to a rise in quality-adjusted demand would result in higher housing expenditure. Expenditure may be measured either as capital cost or as annual mortgage outgoings. Since it is the flow of services from the house that is actually demanded, the latter would seem more appropriate.

Much research has been undertaken to determine the income elasticity of demand for housing [8, 11, 18, 44, 45, 53, 68, 84, 86]. The general opinion is that it is about unity. However, the studies have arrived at a variety of results, so this figure must be used with care. Elasticity varies according to income level, higher income brackets being more responsive than those with incomes of a lower level. Thus, elasticity may vary between areas according to their socio-economic structure.

(c) *Price* Demand would normally be expected to have an inverse relationship to price. However, in the case of the housing market, this is not quite so obvious. For the first-time buyer it seems fairly safe to assume that, as prices rise, demand will fall due to fewer households being able to afford to buy, or their buying lower quality houses. However, a counteracting effect might arise if purchase now rather than later is seen as an inflation hedge, i.e. if the price rise is seen as heralding a period of rising house prices, people may bring forward their buying plans, thus initially preventing demand from contracting.

For owner-occupiers who are moving, the problem is slightly different. Rising prices imply a higher price for the house they are selling as well as for the house they are buying. For example, consider a household on an income of £4000 which has bought a house for £10 000. (For simplicity, we will assume that it has a 100 per cent mortgage and that the building society's lending rate is 2½ times income.) If the household now has to move for reasons of employment, it may sell its house and buy a similar one, for the same price, all else remaining unchanged. Now, assume a 10 per cent rise in prices has occurred. They will sell their house for £11 000, making £1000 capital gain. They may still buy that similar house, now at £11 000, without increasing their monthly outgoings, by using the £1000 capital gain and maintaining a mortgage of £10 000. In this case, being able to reap capital gains prevents any contraction in demand due to higher prices.

On *a priori* reasoning then, market demand may be fairly unresponsive to changes in price. Demand from first-time buyers may react strongly, but this is much less likely for existing owner-occupiers who move, and against this must be set any counteracting tendency due to desires for a hedge against inflation in house prices. Further, we might expect the effects of price changes to be stronger the greater the proportion of first-time buyers in total demand.

The relevant concept of price is price relative to other prices. Further, the buyer will be interested in what he actually has to pay out, thus price should be measured as the cost of the house plus the cost of financing any loan necessary to purchase the house. Either selling prices plus interest costs or annual repayments of mortgage (principal

21

plus interest) may be used. Again, since it is the flow of services which is demanded, the latter would be preferable. Another method, of course, would be to treat the two variables independently — that is, to consider the reaction of demand to house prices and the mortgage rate separately. It has been suggested that the price buyers will consider as having to be paid for the flow of housing services that they buy will include not only the two variables already mentioned but also the cost of rates and maintenance. Logically, the buyer must certainly consider these costs.

The relevant measure of demand should again be in terms of quality-adjusted units, for counting only the number of houses demanded ignores reactions to demand smaller houses in response to a price rise. When estimating income elasticity, it was possible to use expenditure on housing as a measure of quality-adjusted demand; obviously this is not so here. An alternative is to observe how the rateable value of property demanded changes as price changes (on the assumption that rateable values adequately reflect quality). However, most of the studies which have attempted to estimate price elasticity have used only the number of houses demanded, and thus the results are rather unsatisfactory. Much less work has, in fact, been done on price elasticity, and since the method used to measure price has varied quite drastically, drawing general conclusions is risky. Such results as there are suggest an inelastic response to price in the region of -0.7 to -0.5.

(d) *The Availability and Price of Substitutes* As the general level of rents rise, the demand for houses will rise. Little is known about this cross-elasticity, but the presumption is that it is low, since only a small percentage of households are likely to be able to afford to change tenure groups. Of more interest to the current British situation is the availability of rented accommodation. The length and administration of council house waiting lists and the rate of decline in the number of houses available for private renting affects the demand for houses, particularly from newly formed households.

(e) *The Availability of Credit*   Since most households use a loan from a building society in order to purchase their house, the behaviour of these institutions is of interest. Some of their influence has already been included — the effect of rising incomes leading to increased demand may be governed by the societies' lending rules with regard to income as well as the desires of buyers; the effect of the mortgage rate was incorporated into that of price. A third impact may now be added. As is outlined in the next chapter, building societies can only lend out what they receive in the form of savings. If the flow of funds into the societies falls, they must ration a smaller amount of money between buyers by operating their lending rules more stringently. Thus, demand is influenced, via the building societies, by the availability of credit.

(f) *Wealth*   Most people contribute some of the cost of buying their house from their own wealth. Thus, on any given income, the more wealth a household has, the more housing services it can afford to buy. This variable is likely to grow in importance with the growth of owner occupation, which is the most common form of wealth. An existing owner-occupier can use the net proceeds of his sale (the amount of loan he has paid off plus any capital gain) as a down-payment on the purchase of his next house. Thus, the higher the proportion of existing owner-occupiers in total demand, the higher will be the level of quality-adjusted demand for any given income level.

DETERMINANTS OF SUPPLY

Supply consists of existing houses being resold principally by owner-occupiers, and newly built or converted houses being sold by building developers. The supply of second-hand dwellings is not commonly discussed in the literature, but it is possible to make some general deductions about its behaviour from what is known about demand by existing owner-occupiers. Essentially, this source of supply depends upon the rate of mobility of existing owner-occupiers. Households tend to move as they go through the normal cycle of family life or change employment. They may also move in response to changes in their income level, both absolute and relative. They are unlikely to move in response to changes in the house price level. Similarly, the supply of secondhand dwellings is not very responsive to changes in building costs, for there is only an indirect link, through house prices.

The supply of new dwellings responds to a more typical list of factors. Since it takes time to build houses, supply is the result of two critical decisions: the initial decision to start building and decisions on the rate at which the work will be completed. First, factors influencing the level of starts will be considered.

(a) *Price* As prices rise, costs remaining constant, profits rise. Since building developers will respond positively to profits, starts will rise. Although logical in itself, this statement is a simplification for the housing market, because it is rather unlikely that land costs will remain constant in this situation. This point is explained in more detail in Chapter 4, but for the moment it will be ignored. When house building is bespoke, that is, when it is built for a specific individual, on his orders, the price relevant to the builder is the price in the contract. However, most houses for owner occupation are built on speculation, in that they are not put on the market until they are at or near completion. Hence, the price relevant to the builder is the price he can expect to get when the house is completed. Thus, he bases his decision of the level of starts on what he thinks the state of the market will be at some considerable, and to some extent indeterminable, time in the future.

Having expected prices as a determining variable, besides making life difficult for the builder, makes prediction of the relationship between price and number of starts problematic; the use of current price implies imperfect specification. In addition, few studies of supply make any adjustments for housing quality. Not surprisingly, estimates of elasticity vary widely [66, 71, 77]. Since expectations are a critical factor here, an alternative to using price, either current or what it actually turns out to be when the house is sold, as a determining variable is to consider those factors which influence expectations. Possible indicators that building developers might use are the flow of funds into building societies, the level of vacant houses waiting for sale and the length of time it is currently taking to sell new houses.

(b) *Costs*   The relationship between costs and starts will be inverse. As costs rise, prices remaining constant, profits fall and thus builders cut back on starts. The relevant concept of costs may again involve elements of expectations for resources which are used late in the building process. Costs may be split into land costs, pre-construction costs (mostly professional fees), construction costs (labour and materials) and financial costs. The last occur because many building developers borrow money in order to build. These loans are repaid as the builder is paid for his work, but in the mean-time he must pay interest on them.

The responsiveness of supply to a change in any one category of costs will depend upon the latter's proportional share in total costs. This obviously varies as costs change; for example, the proportion of costs used in buying land rose dramatically in the early 1970s and is now falling back, due to fluctuations in the relative price of land. However, in general, construction costs are by far the most significant element and can be expected to exert a strong effect on starts. (Building costs are investigated in more depth in Chapter 4.)

(c) *Availability of Credit*   Since many builders borrow money in order to function, the level of starts is directly related to the availability of credit. This factor is likely to move against the cost of credit, thus reinforcing its effect on the level of starts.

(d) *Availability and Profitability of Other Work*   Building firms operate over a number of markets (Figure 1.1). To the extent to which builders move between markets, conditions prevalent in one market may affect supply in the others. The strength of cross-entry response will, of course, depend upon the degree to which capacity in the industry is being utilised. However, since demand for residential buildings (by both private individuals and local authorities) and demand for non-residential building are both influenced by the cyclical behaviour of the availability and cost of finance, they will peak at the same time and capacity limitations will operate. It has been argued that housing may suffer as a result of this competition for resources [66]. The suggestion is that the price elasticity of supply for non-residential building is greater than that for residential building, and thus when demand in the former market is high, the supply of residential building shifts to the left and becomes more inelastic.

(e) *Seasonal Factors*   For obvious reasons the climate will affect the level of starts. Starts will exhibit a seasonal pattern and haphazard events such as a particularly harsh winter will cause the pattern to vary.

The supply of new dwellings coming on to the market will be determined by the rate at which building proceeds as well as the rate of starts. The time lag between the initial decision to build and release of the building on to the market is considerable and has three main elements: time spent in designing, time spent in obtaining planning permission and time spent on construction. The last, the lag between start and completion, accounts for only 40 per cent of the time lag at the most. These lags can vary widely in length. Difficulty in obtaining planning permission is one factor which will influence supply through its effect on the time lag. The size and complexity of building schemes is another factor which can influence both design and construction time. In the construction phase, bad weather and delays in delivery of material will also have their effect. Apart from these external influences on building time, there is evidence that the construction phase varies in length

26

according to economic conditions. Building exhibits cyclical tendencies and construction times tend to lengthen during slumps and shorten during booms.

To summarise, supply arises from two sources with different motivations. The overall responsiveness of supply to economic variables will depend on the proportions of secondhand and new houses in the total. New houses make up something like 40—50 per cent of the total flow of houses coming on to the market, but this, of course, varies. Thus, for example, the effects of building costs on supply and thus price will be greater the greater the proportion of new houses in supply.

PRICE LEVEL

This is a free market and thus the price level for houses will be determined by the interaction of demand and supply:

Demand = f (income, price, rents, availability of credit, wealth, demographic factors)

Supply = Supply of secondhand houses + Supply of new houses

= f (mobility) + f (price, costs, availability of credit, availability of other building work, seasonal factors, delays in the building process)

Demand = Supply, to determine equilibrium prices

Once these functions have been fully specified it is possible to trace the effects of a change in any determining variable on demand, supply and price, and finally through to the housing stock. However, price adjustment may not occur very rapidly. In such a complex market, demand and secondhand supply tend to be slow to alter their expectations of prices. In addition, because of the existence of a large secondhand market, prices are slow to react to cost changes in new building, thus new and secondhand house prices may diverge. Over the longer run, prices have tended to rise. This trend is explained by reference to rising incomes and consequent rising demand for housing services and, on the supply side, slow improvements in productivity. The latter is analysed in Chapter 4.

RELATIVE PRICES

It is the attributes possessed by a house which are valued by the consumer. Thus, the relative evaluation of a house compared to other houses depends on the degree to which it possesses these attributes and the weight attached to each attribute by consumers. As has already been suggested, these attributes may be classified under two headings: locational or external attributes and dwelling or internal character-istics.

Accessibility is the most commonly considered locational characteristic of housing. Consumers will distinguish between houses according to the ease with which they may travel from them to work, school or the shopping centre. It will be closely influenced by distance, but such factors as quality of roads, public transport services and density of traffic will also be of importance. The level of accessibility is determined by both the time spent on travel and its costs. These two factors may not necessarily move together, but usually do. As time and cost of travelling rise, other aspects of houses being identical, consumers' evaluations will fall, and thus price will be lower. If most of the places to which a household requires access are within the centre of an urban area, we can expect that prices for similar houses will fall with increasing distance from the city centre, though the fall will be less along the main transport routes. Not all consumers will evaluate accessibility in the same way, an obvious example being the difference between a car-owning household and a household that relies on public transport. Thus, the pattern of price differentials due to accessibility will vary between local housing markets according to the population structure of the area, as well as the structural peculiarities of the area, such as its road network.

A second set of locational attributes arises from environmental factors. Consumers will compare houses according to the quality of the neighbourhood in which they are located. When buying a house, the consumer buys the location as well as the physical structure. He can therefore be expected to consider, and evaluate, such things as the quietness of the neighbourhood, the way the neighbourhood keeps its gardens and outside paintwork. the school whose catchment area the house is in, and so on. This creates patterns of price differentials for similar houses, according to the district of the city in which they are located. It has been suggested that the environmental attributes which are desired by buyers may vary according to social class and income. Thus, again, price relatives will vary between cities according to their population characteristics. There are also environmental attributes specific to individual houses which will cause price differences even within a fairly homogeneous district. The house overlooking the cricket field might have a premium, while the one overlooking the sewage works will fetch less than average.

It can frequently be observed that attractive districts tend to be on the outskirts of an urban centre. This may happen for many reasons: the land may be cheaper and therefore buildings are less crowded on the outskirts of town, the centre may contain factories and slum buildings, and so on. This places the buyer in a position where he must trade off accessibility with environmental quality. Where he will choose to settle will depend on his relative evaluation of the two sets of attributes. In terms of prices likely to result from demanders' evaluations, we have two contradictory influences. As distance from the town centre increases, accessibility factors would be expected to push price down, but environmental factors to push it up. The price—distance relationship for similar houses is therefore likely to be a curve rather than a straight line.

Turning now to the attributes of dwellings themselves, the possibilities for differences between houses are endless. Size is a factor which will obviously be considered by buyers, but size is a multi-dimensional concept. Buyers might be interested in plot area, floor area, number of bedrooms, the presence or otherwise of a separate dining room, or the size of the kitchen. These various dimensions of size will not always move together, but in general it is expected that valuation, and thus price, will rise with size. Again, buyers' valuations may be expected to vary; for example, large families will have different preference structures to small ones. Type of house may also be expected to influence valuation. Detached houses may be regarded as more desirable than semi-detached houses, and both as preferable to terraced houses. Buyers are also interested in whether the dwelling is a house, bungalow or flat (and if it is a flat, which floor). The age of the dwelling may also affect its price. The relationship is not simple though; new dwellings require little maintenance and therefore value should decline with age, but many older houses are valued because of their character. The presence or otherwise of amenities such as garage, central heating, second toilet, storage space and kitchen layout, will also be evaluated by buyers and thus cause price differentials.

From what has now been said, it is clear that is is being hypothesised that buyers can place accurate valuations on a multitude of different attributes. If they cannot do so, the price relatives mean very little. It was mentioned at the beginning of this chapter that this was a market where information is costly; we can now see why. One interesting possibility has been put forward by Cubbins [15]. He suggests that because information is so costly, buyers might seek to avoid the cost by using prices as an indicator of quality. In this study, Cubbins found that houses which he regarded as being slightly over-priced in relation to his evaluation of their attributes, took a shorter time to sell. This is the opposite of what might be expected, and thus led to the suggestion that buyers, rather than comparing a mass of different houses for variations in attributes, might rely on price to accurately reflect quality of attributes. He did, however, find a normal relationship between selling time and price when the over-pricing became significantly large.

30

Thus, even though it must be realised that price relatives are subject to anomalies, it is possible to accept a rough relationship between final selling price and attributes.

Over recent years there has been a lot of research concerned to elicit attributes' valuations and thus explain price relatives. Some examples of these studies are contained in the bibliography [2, 15, 24, 29, 43, 44, 53, 69, 87]. Collectively these studies examine a large number of relationships between determining variables and price relatives. Their results have been summarised in the above discussion, but only in terms of the direction of the effect on prices. It is apparent from these studies that many factors influence relative house valuations, no one factor being clearly dominant. Since most studies concentrate on one particular theoretical relationship they fail to provide a general theory, and do predict differing results; in addition, as mentioned in the above paragraph, we would anticipate that results will vary because the market is not perfect. However, not all of the variations may be haphazard. Studies typically use different study areas; thus, results might be expected to differ between studies as population structure differs. Further, since urban structures can vary, the importance of particular attributes varies and thus their effect on relative price formation. For example, the effect of accessibility is likely to be more noticeable in an area where employment is concentrated in the centre than in an area where employment opportunities are dispersed. Finally, given any set of valuations, prices may vary according to supply. The nature of the stock of houses between areas differs for historical reasons. Thus, even in studies where demands are roughly comparable, equilibrating price relatives may vary.

The derivation of price relatives has been discussed in a static manner, but, of course, they will adjust to bring equilibrium in exactly the same manner as the price level. For example, if within one particular area the demand for four-bedroomed, detached houses is larger than supply, it would be expected that houses with these dwelling attributes would rise in price relative to other houses. This change in relative price might act to encourage builders to build more houses of this type. Some demanding household might respond to the relative price change by deciding that a five-bedroomed semi or a three-bedroomed detached house overlooking the park is now better value for its money. Thus, relative price will adjust so that demand and supply move towards equilibrium.

3 Finance for House Purchase

Houses are so expensive that most people who buy them take out a loan in order to do so. This chapter will be concerned with the supply of such loans to private individuals. (Loans to public bodies are discussed in Chapter 5.) Due to the decline in private renting, there is very little demand for finance to buy houses to let; thus, concentration will be on finance for owner occupation. The first section will briefly list the various sources of finance. Since building societies are by far the most important source, the remainder of the chapter will concentrate on their behaviour.

SOURCES OF FINANCE

(a) *Building Societies* These are the only institutions whose primary concern is the finance of house purchase, and they constitute the major source for such finance (Table 3.1).

To borrow money from a building society it is often necessary to have been a shareholder with the society for some small period of time, though this need not involve a large outlay of money. The loan made is a mortgage loan, i.e. money is lent for purchase of a property on security of that property. The normal length of time over which a loan is made is 25 years. The normal method of repayments is the annuity system, i.e. the total cost, principal plus interest, is broken down into constant monthly instalments. Initially, most of this sum will be interest payments and the capital owing will decline slowly. Since tax relief is given on interest payments, the net cost to the borrower rises through time, as the interest element in repayments declines.

TABLE 3.1
Loans for house purchase in the United Kingdom

	Building Society £m	Local authority £m	Insurance company £m	Total £m
1970	2 021	175	154	2 350
1971	2 758	243	148	3 149
1972	3 649	325	149	4 123
1973	3 540	491	258	4 289
1974	2 950	676	249	3 875

Source: *Financial Statistics*, no. 165, Jan 1976 (C.S.O.), Supplementary Table C.

However, historically, this has been more than counteracted by the effect of inflation. Over the length of life of the loan, the constant monetary repayment declines in real value; thus, the real cost of servicing a mortgage declines over time. The building society may vary the rate of interest, both on new and existing loans; therefore monthly repayments are subject to a degree of uncertainty.

The size of loan granted depends on characteristics of the borrower and of the property. Societies operate a rule whereby no more than some multiple (currently 2½—3 times) of the borrower's income is loaned. They may also refuse to take into account incomes other than the basic pay of the head of the household. Further, they may refuse to lend more than some maximum. The second determinant of the loan is the property itself. The property is valued for the society, and the loan is made according to which is the lower — the valuation or the price. The loan will be a percentage of this figure. Societies may be prepared to lend up to 95 per cent on newer property, but only subject to an insurance company guaranteeing the loan in excess of 80 per cent. On older property, the percentage will be less.

(b) *Local Authority Mortgage Services* Local authorities allocate a certain sum of money for the purpose of making mortgage loans each year. This sum is small in relation to the total lent for such purposes, and is specifically for those who experience difficulty obtaining a loan elsewhere. As such, local authorities see themselves as providing a social service rather than as being in competition with building societies. Loans are restricted to cheaper houses and to those whose income makes unlikely the granting of a loan of sufficient size by a building society. It is possible to gain a mortgage which is 100 per cent of the valuation from a local authority, and easier to obtain a mortgage on older property. Thus, this particular source is one that favours the low earners.

(c) *Insurance Companies* Insurance companies do not intend to compete with building societies for the mass of the market for home loans. Rather, they use mortgage facilities as a means of selling endowment policies, which are their principal concern. An individual wishing to finance the purchase of his house with the aid of an insurance company mortgage loan must take out an endowment policy for the same amount as the loan and for the same period of time. During the course of the loan and policy, the borrower pays only the premium on the policy and the interest on the loan. The loan itself is paid off when the policy matures, or the borrower dies. Normally, such loans do not exceed 70 per cent of the valuation of the property.

This method of finance tends to be used by those on higher incomes than average. Two reasons for this may be discerned: the annual repayment of premium and interest is higher, particularly in the early years, than that of a normal building society annuity loan, and insurance companies are more willing to lend on the more expensive properties than building societies. Insurance companies do also operate jointly with building societies in the provision of loans. In such cases, the building society provides the loan and the insurance company the endowment policy.

(d) *Accumulated Savings* Table 3.2 quotes data on building society mortgage loans in relation to the prices of houses they were used to purchase. It can be seen that, on

TABLE 3.2

Building societies: dwelling prices and mortgage advances in the United Kingdom

	Average price £	Average advance £	Average advance as a % of average price %
1970	4 475	3 591	72.2
1971	5 632	4 104	72.9
1972	7 374	5 194	70.5
1973	9 942	6 181	62.2
1974	10 990	6 568	59.8

Source: *Social Trends*, no. 6, 1975 (C.S.O.), Table 4.4.

average, 30—40 per cent of the cost is found from sources other than the building society. The chief secondary source is household wealth. It must be stressed that these are average figures. They include loans made to existing owner-occupiers who are moving. Such households frequently make capital gains on the sale of their old houses; these gains will be used to pay part of the cost of their new houses, thus reducing the percentage size of loan they require from building societies. The average figures will also contain loans made to households that have been in existence for some time or have substantial incomes. Such households may have been able to accumulate savings prior to buying. However, even for first-time buyers who are newly formed households or households on low incomes, some part of the cost is likely to be found from their own wealth. For, with the exception of the local authority mortgage service, financial institutions will not make 100 per cent loans. This last group, who are likely to have low wealth holdings, face a dilemma. To get a high percentage loan, they must buy a newish house, but these houses will tend to be more expensive than older houses of the same size and type.

(e) *Banks* As a rule, banks do not lend money for the purposes considered here. Most households will require a long-term loan and banks prefer to lend over a much shorter period. Their activities are usually restricted to providing bridging loans (short-term loans to bridge the gap between buying a new house and selling the old one) and 'middle-term' loans to individuals in special circumstances. For the average household, banks are unlikely to be of much assistance, though overdraft facilities may well be used extensively to help provide the initial outlay that the household must find for itself.

A few general conclusions can now be drawn about the effect of the finance market on housing. First, the two facts that loans are usually less than 100 per cent and always made in relation to income, can make owner occupation difficult to achieve for those in the lower income groups and first-time buyers, particularly new households. Second, during times of inflation, the normal annuity system places the heaviest burden on the borrower in the early years of a mortgage. This must be compared with the facts that most people are on rising income scales throughout their working life and, in addition, face heavy expenditures of furnishing a house and starting a family in the early years. Consideration has been given to devising more helpful systems of repayment [4, 32, 73]. Third, tax relief on mortgage interest is regressive. The absolute amount of subsidy will rise with the income of the borrower and with the size of his mortgage (and thus the price of house bought). The existence of the subsidy at all, to say nothing of its regressiveness, has been questioned. The system might well be changed following publication of the expected government study, *Review of Housing Finance*. Meanwhile, option mortgages have been introduced to partly redress the balance. Under this scheme, the government pays a subsidy, equivalent to tax relief at normal levels, to building societies, thus enabling them to offer a lower rate of interest to borrowers, providing they do not claim tax relief. The intention is to give an equivalent subsidy to those who pay insufficient tax to enable them to claim full relief.

BUILDING SOCIETIES

(a) *The Movement's Structure* Building societies are private, but non-profit making, bodies. They are run along normal economic lines, although they are increasingly being subjected to governmental pressure to act in certain ways. The movement began in the late eighteenth century, but has experienced rapid growth throughout this century, in line with the expansion of owner occupation. This trend can be seen in Table 3.3. From this table it can also be seen that growth has been accompanied by amalgamation. The movement has developed from its origins of local, self-help groups into one dominated by large, national concerns. Of

TABLE 3.3
Progress of the building society movement

	Number of societies	Total assets £m	Number of borrowers thousands
1900	2 286	60	—
1920	1 271	87	—
1940	952	756	1 503
1960	726	3 166	2 349
1974	416	20 289	4 250

Source: *Facts and Figures*, Jan 1976 (B.S.A.), Table 2.

the 416 societies in existence in 1974, 18 accounted for 80.2 per cent of the movement's total assets. This tendency towards an oligarchic structure is reinforced by the existence of the Building Societies' Association. This is a trade association, important because it recommends to its members the levels of the two vital rates of interest: that paid on shares and deposits and that paid on mortgage loans. These recommendations are widely followed. Such a cartelised structure was common among financial institutions, though its continuance seems odd after 1971, when credit control was introduced in order to encourage competition between banks.

(b) *Behaviour* Building societies act both as savings banks and as financiers of house purchase (Figure 3.1). They function by taking the shares and deposits of small savers, for which they must pay interest, and loaning them out as mortgages, for which they are paid interest. Thus, their principal assets are mortgage loans and their principal liabilities are shares and deposits. Most of their income comes from mortgage interest. This income must cover expenses due to interest payments on shares and deposits, taxation liabilities and management costs, and provide a margin for reserves (this is explained below). Clearly, the amount of money available for mortgages depends upon the flow of funds into building societies from savers. The societies compete for these funds with other institutions. Competition is free, although the societies gain a slight advantage from special arrangements they have with the Inland Revenue for paying savers' taxes [26]. Also, some of their shares are 'captured' because some savers are saving

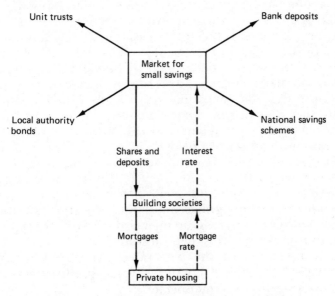

FIG. 3.1   Flow of funds through building societies

specifically for houses and will want mortgages. To maintain their flow of funds at high levels, however, societies must be competitive in terms of the liquidity, security and rate of return they offer savers.

To small savers, ability to withdraw money with little notice is an important attraction. Thus, most institutions who compete for their funds, including building societies, offer easy withdrawal conditions. This makes the societies' main liability extremely liquid, whilst their main assets, mortgages, are illiquid. Since the societies are in this unusual position of borrowing short and lending long, they run the risk of occasionally having more withdrawn than is deposited and consequently not being able to meet their commitments. To protect themselves against this risk, they do not loan out as mortgages all of the money they receive as savings; instead, a percentage will be held as cash and short-term investment. Then, when withdrawals exceed deposits, they can draw on this liquid pool of assets and thus avoid cash flow problems.

A second factor savers will consider when deciding where to put their money is the security of their savings. Thus, building societies compete by creating a reputation for soundness. Savers run the risk of losing some or all of their savings if the assets of the society lose value, i.e. if mortgage default occurs. To reduce the possibility of this, societies try to ensure that they make mortgage loans which are safe. Thus, they operate rules on the quantity of money they are prepared to lend in relation to the borrower's financial circumstances and the value of their security, the house. To cover cases where mortgage default does occur, they hold a pool of reserves. Reserves are, in effect, undistributed profit. Societies operate with a margin between income and expenditure, this margin accumulating over time as a stock of reserves. These reserves can then be depleted to cover asset loss, thus making savers' deposits safe.

The discussion of the past three paragraphs can be summarised in Table 3.4, which gives a simplified picture of how building societies operate.

Competition for funds by means of liquidity and security

TABLE 3.4
Financial operations of building societies

Balance sheet

Liabilities	Assets
1. Shares and deposits	1. Mortgage loans
2. Reserves (undistributed profits which can be used to cover asset loss)	2. Cash and short-term investments (liquid assets)

Revenue and appropriation account

Income	Expenditure
1. Mortgage interest	1. Interest on shares and deposits
	2. Management expenses
	3. Taxes
	4. Additions to reserves

has a number of implications for housing. First, because of the need to hold liquid assets, the amount of money available for mortgages is less, relative to the inflow of funds, than it would be if the inflow was less liquid. Second, because of the need to accumulate reserves, the mortgage rate is higher than it would otherwise be. Finally, because of the need to make secure loans, lending, and thus owner occupation, is restricted to higher income groups and better houses. These implications follow naturally from the need to compete for funds and, anyway, it would be silly to suggest that we try to get more and cheaper mortgages by putting the movement in financial jeopardy. However, it has been suggested that the movement is more cautious than it need be [28, 55]; that it is over-generous in allocating money to liquid assets and reserves and not generous enough in loaning money to borrowers. It has also been suggested that the movement might benefit if it was allowed, and tried, to diversify both assets and liabilities [63].

The third method of competing for funds is the rate of return offered to savers. Given comparable levels of liquidity and security, savers will deposit their money with the institution offering the highest return. Since interest rates are fairly volatile, building societies would need to change the rate offered on shares and deposits quite frequently to maintain their competitiveness and thus their funds. However, when this rate rises, their principal source of expenditure rises. Thus, they must raise more income by raising the mortgage rate. If societies decide to maintain the flow of funds by frequent changes in the two interest rates, they increase management costs (it takes a lot of work to alter mortgage rates) and make the cost of home ownership uncertain, both to existing owner-occupiers who are borrowers and to demanders. The second effect will cause some fluctuation in demand; these short-run fluctuations can disrupt the slow-moving house purchase market.

Due to both the administrative costs of frequent rate changes and governmental pressure to keep the mortgage rate down, building societies do not usually follow this course. Instead, they tend to maintain their rates at constant levels over longish periods of time, and accept fluctuations in their inflow of funds as their competitiveness fluctuates. However, this has in the past created alternating periods of feasts and famines of mortgages. When other interest rates rise, the flow of funds falls and less money must be rationed over those who demand finance by stricter operation of the lending rules; thus, there is less effective demand for houses. Thus, again, the housing market is disrupted by short-run fluctuations in demand, and it seems probable that the disruption is larger than that which would occur if the mortgage rate was allowed to vary.

Governmental pressure to keep the mortgage rate low is questionable, but the costs involved in frequent changes of the mortgage rate are real, so the societies face the problem of how to keep the rate steady without causing instability in the housing market. This issue has received close attention since the house price inflation of 1972, for which the societies were blamed. One suggestion is to create a stabilisation fund into which societies can place spare cash when the inflow of funds is large, which they can then withdraw when the inflow falls, thus enabling them to maintain a steady rate of lending. Societies have not favoured this scheme, probably because they fear government interference with it. Under this threat, however, they are now showing signs of using their liquid assets as stabilising devices. If they allow liquid assets to accumulate during times of plenty and decline during times of shortage, the effect of stability in lending is achieved without the necessity for a formal fund. Success in this, of course, depends upon the size of cycles in the inflow of funds and the chosen level of lending. A long period of low inflows or too high a level of lending will result in inability to maintain stability.

An alternative suggestion [63] is that societies vary the rate on shares and deposits without altering the mortgage rate. This implies fluctuations in the margin allowed for additions to reserves. The dangers are, similarly, a long period of high interest rates and too low a stabilised level of mortgage rate.

(c) *The Mortgage Rate*   The mortgage rate is the price in the market for finance of house purchase. It is not, however, a market determined price: it is determined administratively by the Building Societies' Association. The level of the rate is set on a cost-plus basis. The rate on shares and deposits is dictated by conditions in the financial markets. Once this rate is set, the mortgage rate follows as this rate plus a margin to cover management costs, taxation and additions to reserves necessary to maintain the reserve ratio. Thus, this price does not perform the usual function of allocation, i.e. it does not alter to bring about equilibrium in the demand and supply of mortgages. Instead, allocation is by administrative decision on the part of building societies. They allocate supply across demand according to their assessment of the borrower's security. They will vary the stringency with which they assess security as demand and supply of mortgages varies.

4   New Building

House building was discussed only briefly in Chapter 2, as part of supply coming on to the house purchase market; this chapter will consider it in more detail. The plan is to begin by describing the building industry; this is then followed by discussions on costs, and productivity and design. The final section is concerned with the distribution of building resources between new building and renovation.

THE BUILDING INDUSTRY

The product of the building industry is buildings. This rather obvious statement implies that the industry serves many markets, for the term 'building' covers housing construction (both public and private), construction of buildings for industrial, commercial and leisure use, building of infrastructure such as roads, hospitals and power stations, and the renovation and maintenance of buildings of all types. A breakdown of the industry's output for 1975 is given in Table 4.1. Although individual firms may choose to specialise on one market, the product for the group of markets is sufficiently similar to allow firms to move between them with comparative ease, and to participate in more than one at a time.

Building incorporates three distinct groups of activity: design, manufacture (production of building components) and construction (assembly of the components). The manufacture of building components is much like the rest of manufacturing industry, but design and construction activities are client initiated — that is, work is only undertaken when a contract is placed by a client. The process

TABLE 4.1

The building industry (Great Britain): value of output in 1975

				£m	£m
New housing	:	public		1 483	
	:	private		1 528	
Other new work	:	public		2 525	
	:	private	:	industrial	1 295	
			:	commercial	1 314	
Total new work					8 144
Repair and maintenance	:	housing		1 654	
	:	other public		1 229	
	:	other private		540	
Total repair and maintenance					3 422
Total all work					11 566

Source: *Housing and Construction Statistics*, no. 16, 1975 (H.M.S.O.), Table 5.
Note: Discrepancies in totals are due to rounding.

begins with the client or building owner; he may commission work for his own use or, as a developer, to sell. Either way, he must first buy the plot of land on which the building is to be erected; he is then likely to seek 'outline' planning permission for the intended building. Next, the design plans for the building must be drawn up; this may be done by staff employed by the building owner or, under contract, by professionals such as architects. The resultant plans must then be submitted to the local authority for 'detailed' planning permission. This pre-construction phase of building takes considerable time, longer than the actual construction phase. The time, of course, varies according to the peculiarities of the individual building development and with the occurrence of any delays in the process. (This is discussed in [20] and [56], p. 35. See also Table 4.3.)

Once the plans have been passed, the building owner, if he is not a builder himself, will commission a main contractor to organise the assembly of the building. It is rare for the main contractor to undertake all of the construction work himself; a greater or smaller porportion will be sub-contracted to other builders. This is because construction includes a large number of crafts — *Housing and Construction Statistics*, no. 10, 1974 (H.M.S.O.), Supplementary Table 20, quotes twenty different crafts as being employed in construction. For each craft the work is discontinuous and a small proportion of the total. It would thus be inefficient for one firm to employ all the relevant skills; instead, firms tend to specialise in trades rather than types of building, and subcontracting is thus prevalent.

The construction phase has remained craft based, and therefore labour intensive, despite attempts to mechanise it. The level of capitalisation has remained low and fixed costs in general tend to be low, for much of the labour is hired for the period of the contract only. Low fixed costs, the degree of subcontracting and the variety in size of contracts (from large-scale building such as power stations, down to tiny repair jobs) allow small firms to exist happily along-side the giants. In fact, very small firms predominate, as can be seen from Table 4.2. Further, such small firms tend to move in and out of the industry rapidly. In short, the

TABLE 4.2
Size distribution of firms in the construction industry (Great Britain), in 1973

Number of employees	Number of firms
0— 1	29 563
2— 7	43 962
8— 13	9 311
14— 24	6 315
25— 34	2 364
35— 59	2 298
60—299	2 312
300 and more	451
	96 576

Source: *Housing and Construction Statistics*, no. 10, 1974 (H.M.S.O.), Supplementary Table 16.

industry has a rather fluid form. It is regarded as a rather risky one; the necessity for buildings to be constructed *in situ*, the variety in size and type of contract, the uncertainty of their occurrence, the problems of organising such a large array of trades and arranging for components to arrive at the right time, all make this a difficult industry to run efficiently.

COSTS OF NEW HOUSING

Any breakdown of the costs of building houses must be used with care, for they vary widely with the type of house and its location. In addition, of course, the breakdown will change as individual component prices change. Bearing this in mind, the National Building Agency [56] quotes a notional breakdown of 19 per cent on land and legal costs, 4 per cent on professional design fees and 77 per cent on construction costs (Table 4.3).

Land is a rather special resource and its rapid rise in price during the early part of this decade has brought it much attention. It is characterised by a strong price inelasticity of supply for, though land in general is not particularly scarce, the land of importance for house building is that in or near urban centres which has outline planning permission, and this is limited. Thus, when demand for houses is high, as during the early 1970s, the concomitant high demand for land is met by an inelastic supply, causing its price to soar. The effect is that land costs rise as a percentage of total costs; this puts pressure on house prices but it also means that the rising profit margins of builders are eaten into. When house prices rise in response to rising demand, builders should be stimulated to increase their rate of starts because of higher rates of profit. If, however, land costs rise faster than house prices, that extra profit is shifted from the builder to the land owner, and the stimulus to increase supply is damped.

Two bodies have been blamed for the land price explosion of the 1970s: the local authorities and land owners. Local authorities can make land more scarce than it

47

TABLE 4.3
The house-building process

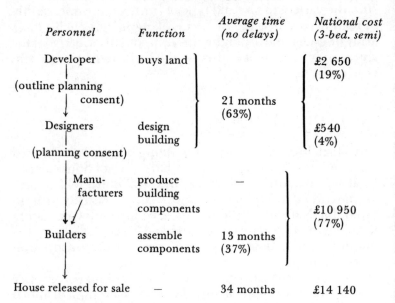

Personnel	Function	Average time (no delays)	National cost (3-bed. semi)
Developer ↓ (outline planning consent) ↓	buys land	} 21 months (63%)	} £2 650 (19%)
Designers ↓ (planning consent)	design building		£540 (4%)
Manu- facturers ↓	produce building components	—	} £10 950 (77%)
Builders ↓	assemble components	13 months (37%)	
House released for sale	—	34 months	£14 140

Source: *Trends in Housing and Construction*, 1976 (N.B.A.), pp. 27, 35.

need be if they are chary of assigning development status to enough land in their area to meet future demand. This is a problem of having not only enough development land at any one time, but also of ensuring an adequate flow of development land to replace that being used up, i.e. it is a planning problem. Apart from complaining that the authorities do not plan far enough in advance, we must also recognise that there are trade-offs between cheap housing and such things as green belt policies and pleasantly planned towns.

Quite apart from difficulties in local authority planning, urban land will remain fairly scarce by its nature. This creates opportunities for land speculation. Where land prices are expected to rise, land owners may find it in their interest to hold on to their property rather than sell it now, in the hope of gaining more in the future. Thus, the supply of land contracts and puts further pressure on the price. Two recent Acts — the Community Land Act and the Development Land Tax Act — have been introduced to try to remove these problems of land supply. It is too early to comment upon them, since both were enacted in 1976, but briefly they envisage local authorities as holding land banks which may be used for development. The authorities will have considerable powers in acquiring land, at current 'use value', at a rate they think necessary. Further, land owners will be subject to tax on both land left undeveloped and land sold for development at high prices.

Construction is by far the most important element in total costs. A very general breakdown of this is 40 per cent on labour, 40 per cent on materials and 20 per cent on profits and overheads (this is a rough split, quoted for guidance only). As might be expected from what has already been said about the nature of the industry, labour costs are a very important factor. The importance of construction costs, plus the difficult nature of the industry, have led to extensive efforts to find ways of improving construction or reducing its importance in building. It is to this we now turn.

PRODUCTIVITY AND DESIGN

Productivity in the building industry has been increasing, but at a slower rate than in manufacturing industry. The explanation for this lies in the lack of technological break-throughs and mechanisation which have been responsible for the gains in efficiency achieved by manufacturing industry [5, 25, 80]. The effect is that housing costs have risen, relative to the price of other goods. Construction, the most costly part of building, has remained labour intensive. The high proportion of craft work and the small and irregular occurrence of any particular task in the construction process, make it unconducive to mechanisation. Machines, to be used effectively, require tasks which are

49

simple and repetitive. If mechanisation cannot be used in construction, the alternative is to use modern methods by using prefabricated units — that is, to reduce the on-site construction element in building by increasing the manufacturing element. To some extent, prefabrication has proved cost effective, but this is not true for the more bulky building components. For the latter, transport costs are high; the units are awkward to move about and the distance to be travelled is longer (source to factory to building site rather than source to site). Second, in Britain, the relative costs of labour and machines have been against making prefabrication cost effective in many cases.

If productivity cannot be improved by extending the use of capital, perhaps there is scope for improving it by better organisation of men and materials. Building is structured such that there is a definite split between the pre-construction and construction phases. It has been claimed that this division can cause inefficiency through a lack of knowledge on the part of designers of the problems and innovations in construction. Thus, their plans are not designed to minimise construction costs, and more co-ordination between the two could give efficiency gains. Within the construction phase itself, organisation of men and materials is a complex job with much scope for inefficiency. The employment of skilled on-site managers and careful pre-planning could also improve productivity.

The alternative to looking for productivity gains to reduce the high cost of building is to design houses which are cheap. Where land is becoming scarce and expensive, increasing the density of building is one way to prevent houses rising in price. One search for a solution along these lines was in the development of high rise buildings. This has not always proved successful and has now been largely abandoned. It is not as economical on land use as might be supposed, for open land around a tall building is necessary for adequate lighting, and recreation areas are necessary for children living in flats. Hence, the gains in reduced land costs are not great, and must be set against considerable rises in construction costs. High rise blocks require expensive materials and techniques to build, and facilities such as lifts must be added. Thus, building upwards is not often cost effective and, in addition, has been shown to have undesirable social effects on the people who must live there. A more profitable way of increasing density is to reduce plot size. Traditional houses can be built with smaller gardens, thus providing clear savings in costs. Building terraced houses rather than other types of traditional dwellings also provides land savings, though these are not great.

Construction costs may also be lowered by building terraces, since these costs rise with size, though by no means proportionately. There are also some economies of scale in construction from building estate developments rather than individual houses or small groups of houses. Further, standard designs and designs which consider factors such as the size of building components when determining room sizes can reduce construction costs. Finally, building costs can be lowered if standards are lowered. Most private house building is regulated by the National Housebuilding Council and many council houses are built to reach Parker—Morris standards. The latter, in particular, give very high quality housing with regard to storage and living space. It is unfortunately true that setting such high standards must restrict the number of council houses which can be built from any given budget. The trade-off between standards and cost needs to be recognised [65].

Determining the desirability of building cheap houses is a complex question, for houses built now will last a long time. If, as has been true in the past, expectations rise, cheap houses may become socially obsolete long before they are technically so. Perhaps we have paid too much attention to the necessity element in housing by wanting to keep the cost down. Housing does have large luxury elements for most people and perhaps they would prefer to spend a growing proportion of income on housing in order to conserve quality.

IMPROVING THE HOUSING STOCK

House building has two effects: it may add to the quantity of housing in the stock and it may improve the quality of the stock by replacing obsolete houses with new ones. Additions to the stock cater for the homeless and for population growth. Replacement of the stock is always necessary, as individual houses age. Since a basic aim of society is to house its members in accommodation of reasonable standard, these two effects are regarded as beneficial. However, this view must be examined with care. Newly built houses tend to be of the highest quality with regard to their general condition and amenities. They thus command relatively high prices and are occupied by the higher income groups. As houses age, they deteriorate and become socially obsolete in their layout and amenities. Their relative prices fall and they become available to successively poorer sections of the population — this, of course, is a general tendency only. Demolishing the oldest and poorest accommodation therefore displaces relatively poor households. These households will not be able to afford the new accommodation which replaces the slums. By a similar line of argument, expanding the housing stock to meet the needs of growing household formation is again providing expensive new houses for a section of the population which contains many fairly low income households.

In theory, this need not necessarily matter, for houses should filter down. That is, the more wealthy households will be encouraged to move to new, high-quality accommodation. As they do so, they will free the houses they had previously occupied, now relatively cheaper, for those lower down the income scale. As filtering occurs, new households and those displaced from the slums should find better quality, older houses coming within their means. Filtering depends for its success upon the existence of the right conditions. Households must be highly mobile if the process is not to take considerable time. Second, prices for the existing stock must fall relatively, i.e. there must be no excess demand at any stage in the process to halt it. Third, it is necessary for prices to fall faster than quality for these households to be any better off. Much depends upon the age structure of the stock and the distribution of households throughout the income scale (for a deeper analysis, see [24] and [51]). In short, filtering alone cannot be relied upon to provide good accommodation for the poorest. Further, in relation to the clearance of slum areas, the density of housing removed tends to be greater than that which replaces it. Thus, more households will be displaced from the land than can be re-accommodated.

New building specifically for poorer households and those displaced by slum clearance has been created through the activities of local authorities in building council estates. This method does require considerable subsidisation, however. The alternative way of directly providing good accommodation for these groups is to use building resources to renovate old houses, rather than build new ones.

Obsolescence can be delayed by renovation, thus reducing the need for clearance and replacement and providing housing of an acceptable standard in the lower price ranges. Since building resources are scarce, there is a trade-off between new building and renovation. This is not a simple decision to take; replacement can only be delayed and thus some resources must be devoted to it. The extent to which renovation is desirable depends upon a comparison of costs and benefits. On the cost side, it is necessary to compare the costs of renovation and rebuilding in relation to the length of life of renovated and newly built property. On the benefit side, comparisons must be made between the quantity and quality of housing services derived from renovated and new houses over the relevant time periods, and possibly consideration should also be given to who get the benefits. Some research has been undertaken in this area; in particular, Needleman has attempted to derive a method to indicate when renovation would be preferable to rebuilding. For a further discussion of this issue the reader is referred to his work and some comments made upon it [57, 58, 59, 74, 75].

The desirability of renovation has so far been treated on an academic plane. In the real world, it may be expected to occur as individual house owners make decisions to demand resources for improvements and repairs. They will make their decisions in terms of their own, private, costs and benefits. However, the government has taken the view that the implications are wider than the strictly private, and operates a system of subsidising renovation. There are a variety of improvement grants offered, but basically they give, to house owners, a percentage of the cost of modernisation up to some maximum. Houses must have a minimum life remaining to qualify, and there are conditions as to the types of modernisation which can gain subsidy. Grants must be applied for; thus the basic decision to renovate remains a private one. In some ways, this is not the most desirable situation. Private decisions might not allocate the money for subsidies across the housing stock in an optimal manner. However, in general, the policy seeks to ensure that the stock contains a proportion of houses of 'reasonable' standard, but within the lower price ranges.

5 The Market for Rented Accommodation

The market for rented accommodation will be analysed in a manner similar to that used in Chapter 2, except that the small, luxury end of the market will be ignored. Since many of the definitional points are the same, the details will not be repeated here. The time period over which behaviour is analysed is the short run (except in the second section, where the long run period is also discussed), and the relevant market is the local one. Heterogeneity again implies the use of quality-adjusted units and the existence of both a general level and relative rents. Finally, demand and supply are market functions, measured as flows.

There are few institutions which assist the workings of this market. In the private sector, estate agents may be used but much more stress is placed upon personal search through such things as local newspapers and informal contacts. Similarly, solicitors and accountants may be consulted, but this need not be so. Hence, there is potential for participants to be badly informed and face search difficulties. The public sector has only one local supplier, the local authority. Demand is registered simply by joining their waiting list, but allocation of a house is an administrative decision that may involve considerable delay and little choice.

DETERMINANTS OF DEMAND

(a) *Price* The demand for rented accommodation will have an inverse relationship to rent. As real rents rise, the rate of household formation may fall and the incidence of multi-occupation rise; both responses will reduce demand. A response to demand smaller and poorer accommodation will also cause quality-adjusted demand to contract. Finally, some households may be in a position where they can respond by opting to buy rather than rent. The degree of responsiveness to price is likely to be lower than that of owner-occupiers, for lack of income and wealth may prevent many households from choosing to buy rather than rent, and the fact that much of the supply of rented accommodation is administratively controlled may prevent households from choosing smaller and poorer accommodation or sharing accommodation.

The relevant concept of rent is not unambiguously clear. To some demanders, rent may be quoted as inclusive of rates and repairs. To others, either or both expenditures will be in addition to rent. To provide a measure common to both, it is therefore suggested that rent be defined as inclusive of rates and repairs. The concept should be further refined to rent relative to other prices. In Britain, a system of rent rebates and allowances exists. These are subsidies towards the cost of accommodation which are paid by the state to households, according to their economic circumstances. In a way, they are the counterpart to the tax relief given to owner-occupiers, and households might be expected to consider them to arrive at a net rent upon which they base their decisions. However, unlike tax relief, rent subsidies are not granted automatically. Information about them is poor and take-up is suspected to be low [46]. Thus, many demanders may make their decisions without regard to them.

Empirical research on the behaviour of the British rented sector is scant, and much of the evidence from America is inapplicable. This problem, of course, must be added to the usual one of difficulty in measuring in quality-adjusted units. With even more scepticism than usual, therefore, we may say that the evidence is that the price elasticity of demand is less than one.

(b) *Income*   The relevant concept of income is the real,

permanent, net-of-tax income of the main breadwinner. At low levels of income, demand will rise with it. Household formation may rise, the incidence of multi-occupation fall and households may choose better and bigger accommodation. However, the latter response is inelastic, since housing at this level is regarded as a necessity. Above a certain level of income, demand is likely to contract, for rented accommodation becomes an inferior good to owner occupation.

(c) *Wealth*   Owner occupation is typically regarded as a state superior to renting accommodation, the principal barriers to achieving the preferred state being insufficient income and/or wealth. Thus, it is expected that as individual wealth accumulates, demand for rented accommodation falls.

(d) *Prices of Other Goods*   As the price of home ownership rises relative to the price of renting, demand for rented accommodation will rise. The main effect of this factor will be on would-be first-time buyers, who find themselves unable to afford to purchase and therefore opt to enter the rented market. The same effect is expected to result from a reduction in the availability of mortgages.

(e) *Availability of Rented Accommodation*   This factor must be added to the usual list of factors determining demand, since the majority of the market is controlled such that rent is below its market level. In this situation, excess demand is predicted and will manifest itself in waiting lists for council houses and difficulty in finding privately rented units. Under such conditions, demand might well respond by contracting as would-be demanders are deterred from entering the market and opt instead for owner occupation or multi-occupation. Thus, as waiting lists lengthen and time spent in search of privately rented accommodation increases, demand will fall.

(f) *Demographic Factors*   As was mentioned in Chapter 2,

the rate of household formation, employment opportunities and the distribution of families over their life-cycle
will affect demand. A fourth, not strictly demographic,
factor might be included here, that of the occupational
distribution within a locality. Choice between renting and
owner occupation depends not only on the strictly
economic factors so far considered, but also on social class
and tenure choice of parent. A family history of tenure
preference seems to be perpetuated to some extent.

DETERMINANTS OF SUPPLY — PRIVATE SECTOR

Supply from both sectors will consist of houses from the
stock of rented accommodation which have become
available for reletting as existing tenants move, and
additions to the stock which are being let for the first time.
The flow from the former source will depend upon the
mobility of existing tenants. However, in the private sector
this is not the only determinant, for once a property falls
vacant, the landlord has the option to relet or to take the
property off the market. He will base his decision on
economic factors similar to those he will use when deciding
whether or not to increase the stock of rented accommodation. These factors are listed below.

Before considering them, however, it is necessary to say
something about the motivations of landlords. The
function of rentier is undertaken by a variety of bodies:
profit-oriented companies, housing associations who seek
only to cover costs and individuals, not necessarily well off,
who may own as little as one rented unit — historically, it
has been the small landlords who have been numerically
more important. Not surprisingly, their motivations vary.
Thus, the list of factors deemed to determine supply is an
amalgam; to any individual landlord the importance of
each factor will depend upon his motivation. Companies
and housing associations will typically be interested in the
income and cost flows arising from renting. Even where this
is true to individuals, the net income for renting is fre-

quently secondary to their earned income. However, individuals may also rent out houses they have bought as a means of storing wealth in a way which is protected from inflation. In this case, it is the value of the asset and ability to sell it which are of dominant interest. Some individuals rent out accommodation purely as a temporary arrangement, in order to keep the property occupied whilst they are away from it. Or they may rent out part of their house in order to cover some part of mortgage costs they incur as owner-occupiers. These latter two groups might not seek to cover costs.

(a) *Income* Net income to the landlord is rent less costs and taxes. Costs consist of a service element and a capital element. Service costs include those expenses incurred in the management and repair of property owned. Capital costs may be mortgage costs, or opportunity costs if the property is owned outright. Tax must be paid on income, net of allowable costs. Landlords are in the unusual position of not being able to count asset depreciation as a cost. For tax purposes, a house is deemed an immortal asset. Thus, landlords face a high tax burden compared to most other businesses, and there is little incentive for them to maintain or improve their property. The landlord, like the owner-occupier, may offset interest costs against income. However, he can only offset them against income from the property itself. By comparison, the owner-occupier may offset interest costs against his total income and is not taxed on imputed rental income anyway.

Rents are not freely determined. Since 1915, there has been some sort of government policy in existence whose aim has been to hold rent levels below their market value. Until 1965, these policies were intended as temporary expediency measures during times of crisis (particularly wars). However, in 1965, when the rent regulation machinery was set up, control was recognised as being of a permanent nature. (The regulation machinery was intended for unfurnished tenancies by the 1965 Rent Act; its field was extended to include furnished accommodation by the 1974

Rent Act. These and other related Acts are explained in more detail in [78].) The aim of rent regulation is to create a system of 'fair rents'. This is a rather ambiguous term to the economist, but, briefly, rent levels are to be set as though there were no shortage of supply; thus giving only a 'fair' return to the landlord. Relative rents are to be determined according to each property's individual characteristics. Landlord and tenant must agree a rent, which is registered with the rent officer. Any disagreement may be taken to rent assessment committees. Renegotiation may take place only after a lapse of three years. Prior to 1965, controlled rents had failed to keep pace with inflation. Since then they have been allowed to rise, but only slowly.

On *a priori* reasoning, it would be expected that supply would rise with real net income. Thus, it is predicted that as real rents rise, supply rises, but only in so far as net-of-tax income from rents rises. As real costs and tax rates rise, supply contracts. Looking first at the long run, the secular decline in privately rented accommodation is partly explained by falling real rents, due to rent control and relatively high tax costs, due to the landlord's unusual tax position. The response to these trends has been in terms of both numbers and quality of rented accommodation. In the short term, rising rents under regulation might stimulate supply, but the response is likely to be inelastic because of fear that regulation could once again fail to keep pace with inflation. Rising costs will produce a more responsive cutback in supply because landlords are unable to offset many of them for tax purposes.

(b) *Asset Value* Since one of the motivations for owning rented property is in order to store wealth, its attractiveness will depend on it maintaining or improving its real value. Over its life, a house will lose value, but in the short run houses have, historically, been inflation-proof assets. Thus, it might be expected that, where house prices are expected to rise in real terms, the supply of rented accommodation will increase. There are, however, factors militating against such a reaction. First, because of the tax position of the land-

60

lord with regard to improving his property, rented houses depreciate faster than houses in general. Second, the landlord is subject to tax on capital gains made by selling his property, thus softening the stimulus to supply from any real price rises. Finally, legislation to give security of tenure has the side-effect of reducing the value of the landlord's asset. Property sold with vacant possession is worth more than that sold with sitting tenants. The landlord must therefore either take a lower price or wait until his tenants have moved in order to sell rather than sell at his convenience. Thus, when expectations of real house prices rise, the supply of rented accommodation does not respond very strongly. In fact, the introduction of security of tenure legislation has had a significant response in other directions and is another factor contributing to the long-term decline of rented accommodation.

(c) *Alternatives to Renting*   Renting property is a means of obtaining income and storing wealth. The supply of rented accommodation may therefore be expected to have an inverse relationship with returns to be had from other methods of obtaining the same. For some landlords who are investors rather than entrepreneurs, the alternative may be in capital market, and the rise of the latter is yet another factor involved in explaining the long-term decline in the supply of rented accommodation. Assets in this market may yield extremely competitive returns, without all the trouble involved in managing rented property. For many of the smaller landlords, the alternatives lie in the various pension and savings schemes now in existence. Again, over the long run, these alternatives have been created and made inflation-proof, thus reducing the supply of rented accommodation.

(d) *Availability of Finance*   The landlord as entrepreneur will need to borrow money in order to buy houses to rent. Apart from the Housing Corporation, which lends to housing associations, there is no institutionalised system for lending to rentiers. (The Housing Corporation was set up under the 1964 Housing Act as a source of finance to housing societies who provide cost-rent and co-ownership accommodation. Societies may borrow (on a 40-year loan) part of the cost of building from the corporation, the remainder being obtained from building societies in the normal manner. Note, however, that the corporation can only lend to these non-profit making societies, and that such societies currently rent only a very small percentage of the stock of rented accommodation.) Building societies prefer to lend for owner occupation and rentiers have never entered the capital market in the way most other businesses have done. To be able to charge a rent competitive with owner occupation or council housing, the landlord needs to borrow money on very long loans (local authorities borrow for 60 years). Few bodies are willing to do this. Thus, lack of finance, or to put it another way, the failure of landlords to adapt to modern business conditions, is the final factor in explaining the long-term decline in private renting.

Over this section, attention has been paid to the long-run movements in supply, rather than the short run used throughout the rest of this book. Factors contributing to this effect are numerous. Some are government caused: rent control, security of tenure and the position of landlords. However, a downward movement would have occurred even without this direct interference; lack of financial sources, the rise of the capital market and the creation of pensions and savings schemes would have curtailed supply. On the demand side, rises in real incomes and the rise in the building society movement were natural trends that reduced demand. The result of these long-term occurrences is that the privately rented sector is now small and contains accommodation of poor standard. The people who live in this sector tend to be, similarly, poor. Within this picture of long-run decline, short-run movements of real income, real asset value and alternative sources of making money will be expected to have their normal effect directionally. Responsiveness in an upward direction is, however, very weak.

DETERMINANTS OF SUPPLY — PUBLIC SECTOR

The public sector consists of houses owned by local authorities, new town corporations and, in Scotland, special housing associations. This section will be restricted to local authority behaviour, though much of what will be said applies to all three. The purpose of public sector housing has varied, but in general the intention has been to cater for housing needs, somehow defined. Need has not been seen purely in terms of shortage; there have been elements of poverty relief in the aim of providing cheap accommodation for lower income groups and elements of merit goods in the aim of providing high quality accommodation. Movement of population from overcrowded urban areas into overspill towns has also fallen under the general heading of housing needs. In order to meet these needs, public sector housing is administratively controlled, rather than subject to market forces.

Local authorities have rather vague statutory responsibilities to consider housing needs in their area with respect to providing additional accommodation, paying particular attention to situations of overcrowding and unsatisfactory living conditions. Further, they must ensure that those displaced by clearance schemes are adequately rehoused. Within this general framework, authorities are free to act independently. They set their own criteria for assessing needs, building, selecting tenants and charging rent. Thus, the behaviour of public sector supply varies across local authorities. Obviously needs do vary, but more than that, local authority behaviour depends upon its political colour, financial position and inherited stock. The only form of control by central government is that exercised in the granting of subsidies and permission to borrow. Therefore, what follows is a general picture of the behaviour of public sector supply.

Supply again consists of houses being relet and additions to the stock being let for the first time. Supply from the former source depends upon tenant mobility and the size of the local authority's stock; this varies between authorities as the result of historical decisions. Supply from the latter source is determined by current administrative decisions. Thus, only the latter reflects current needs. Factors affecting this supply are considered below. These factors determine the macro public sector supply. On a micro level, council houses, new and old, are allocated according to individual needs. A discussion of this follows.

(i) *Supply of New Houses*

(a) *Assessed Need*   The decision to add to the stock of council housing is generally based on the perceived needs of the locality. These needs may be a crude shortage of number of households over number of houses, in general, or for particular types. In such cases, the need may be perceived through homelessness and overcrowding or through anticipated urban growth. Even without such shortages, need may be deemed to exist in that some units of accommodation currently occupied are unsatisfactory or too expensive for the families they house. The term 'need' is an extremely vague one that depends upon what is viewed as an acceptable state. Not surprisingly, different local authorities use different definitions. Further, information about need may vary; some authorities may look no further than the length of their waiting lists, whilst others may use surveys of the housing stock and local population and predictions of urban movements. In short, although we know that the decision to build is related to need, it is a difficult relationship to predict. At its worst, need is a limitless concept, and there is no body sitting over local authorities to determine relative priorities between them.

(b) *Finance and Costs*   The ability of local authorities to meet needs depends upon their ability to build and to finance their building. Council estates are built by private contractors bespoke to local authorities. The building is financed by 60-year loans borrowed, at market interest rates, from the open market or from the Public Works Loan Board. The only restriction to borrowing money is that permission must be sought from central government. This is

64

usually granted, although permission may be withheld for aggregate demand—management reasons. Apart from this, ability to build will be influenced by capacity limitations in the construction industry and the availability of finance; both tend to be cyclical variables.

Although not run on market criteria, local authority housing must balance its books. Thus, decisions to add to the stock are influenced by ability to pay for new building. The financial situation of local authority housing is shown in the housing revenue account, the main elements of which are shown in Table 5.1. The decision to build more housing will increase expenditure through increased loan charges. The size of the increase will depend on the cost of building and the cost of financing the loan (particularly important for 60-year loans when rates of interest are high). Local authorities receive a government subsidy towards the cost of new building. Historically, there has always been a subsidy system of some sort, though it has varied in nature. At present, we are operating under a holding act, pending a government review [21]. Thus, the situation may change, but currently the cost of new building to the local authority is cushioned by government subsidy. Eligibility for the subsidy depends on the building programme falling within a cost yardstick determined by central government and meeting Parker—Morris standards. Apart from this, the subsidy is given regardless of comparative need between local authorities; all receive the subsidy provided they build to the right specifications.

The remainder of the cost must be met, together with service charges, from rents, rates and any other subsidies to which the local authority is eligible. The new building will

TABLE 5.1
Local authority housing revenue account

Expenditure	*Income*
Loan charges	Rents
Service costs	Government subsidies
	Rate fund contributions

generate extra rental income, but authorities do not set individual rents according to individual costs. Instead, the cost of new housing will be spread over all tenants, and a rate fund contribution may also be made. Authorities are free to determine both rents and rates, but willingness to increase them in order to build is likely to be influenced by what is regarded as reasonable and politically feasible.

In summary, it can only be by the supply of newly acquired stock which is related to current needs and, even here, need must be tempered by ability to finance building. If for a moment we look at the public sector as a whole, rather than at individual local authorities' behaviour, the connection with need grows more remote. Housing problems tend to be local in nature, thus needs vary across the nation, but there is no allocation of central government assistance according to the relative needs of different areas. The subsidy system has never been designed to meet local priorities; currently it provides only a general stimulus to building.

(ii) *Allocation of Local Authority Housing*

Council houses are allocated to individual tenants according to administrative decisions, rather than through price. Households express demand by requesting that their names be added to the waiting list. This is usually open to all, although in some areas prospective tenants may be required to have lived or worked in the area for a period of time before they will be considered. The authority will require information from the applicant as to his circumstances and will visit him at home. The process varies across authorities; sometimes the household's preference for house type are given prominence, sometimes it is the authority's assessment of what they should have which is recorded. Either way, priority on the waiting list will depend upon the individual local authority's allocation criteria. Authorities must give high priority to those displaced by clearance schemes and those living in overcrowded or insanitary conditions; apart from these groups applicants are ranked as each authority sees fit. The criteria they use are sometimes published, sometimes kept secret. The Culling-worth report [16] isolated three broad types of ranking used (see also [70]):

(a) *Rank by Date of Request* This is a first-come-first-served criterion, only really suitable for areas where there is no real shortage, i.e. where the waiting list is short and there are no needy groups. In such situations, it is a system which is easy to operate and seen to be fair.

(b) *Rank by Merit* Under this system, an officer or committee of the authority ranks applicants according to the merit of their case for being allocated a house. The criteria used are obviously informal, and depend on the views of the assessors. Such freedom may be abused or may provide flexibility for consideration of immeasurable needs, and of rare circumstances.

(c) *Rank by Points Schemes* Points schemes are formalised merit schemes. Weights are assigned to types of need, and an applicant's rank is determined by the sum of his weights. The types of need considered will vary from a basic list of purely physical housing circumstances to extensive lists including factors of economic and social wherewithal and length of time in which the applicant has been in need. Weights, similarly, vary through time and between authorities. These schemes are difficult to devise and administer and may become inflexible, but they do represent a more rational formal approach to allocation according to need.

Once ranked on the waiting list, the applicant must wait his turn. The length of time involved is dependent not only on his ranking. In general, the time lengthens with the length of the waiting list and against the mobility of existing tenants. In particular, the time involved will depend upon the demand and supply for houses of the particular type required. The applicant may be able to specify the type of house he wants; he is also free to turn down a house offered to him and request another, though this might not endear him to the authority. However, basically, the authority selects the particular house for the tenant. From the houses they have available, the authority will match house and applicant for size and location. Some authorities may take the matching process further; they may try to assign the poorest applicants to the cheaper estates, and some tend to assign the best housing to those they regard as upright people or likely good tenants.

It can thus be seen that, on the micro level, there is a deliberate attempt to let need determine allocation of supply, though the approach adopted may vary from an attitude of service to the paternalistic. Whatever the merits of the basic aim of the system, it does produce some less desirable side-effects. First, problems may arise over questions of population mobility. Mobility may be hindered by residential qualifications for eligibility to council housing, long waiting lists and difficulty of moving within the public sector, but across local authority boundaries. To the extent that it is, the economy experiences difficulty in adapting to changing employment patterns. Allocation rules also imply difficulty for the highly mobile groups of society, particularly young people such as students. They may not be in one place long enough to buy, yet the likelihood of their obtaining council housing is remote. Second, the allocation system implies a lack of choice to demanders; the authority itself makes the major decisions. Further, council housing tends to be rather uniform and drab, and until recently the majority of it was three-bedroomed houses. Possibly resources could have been used to produce higher levels of consumer satisfaction if the units constructed were more varied and demanders allowed an element of choice between them. Finally, there is the question of social mix. Allocation by need may create areas which contain only low-income families. The desirability of singling these groups out and herding them together may be questionable.

(iii) *Rents*

Throughout the public sector, rents play a minor role, since they do not perform their usual function of allocation. Rents are set administratively by the local authority at a 'reasonable' level. Again, the process is not easy to rationalise in terms of economics, but basically they are related to historic costs. Balancing the Housing Revenue Account implies that income has only to cover service charges and historic loans charges (the latter being by far the largest expenditure). If for a moment we ignore rate fund contributions, total income from rent must then cover historic costs, net of subsidies. Rent levels are set in order to do this. This implies a system known as 'pooling', whereby all tenants pay rent towards costs, regardless of the actual level of historic costs for the particular houses they occupy. In general, this results in tenants of older property paying more than the loan charges for their particular houses and tenants of new property paying less. This should not be taken as implying that tenants in older property pay more than they 'should' do. Rent levels, based on historic costs, are less than market rents and also probably less than they would be under a system of marginal cost pricing, which is usually advocated in other parts of the public sector. The use of historic costs at all is rather questionable, though it must be recognised that income levels are lower in this sector and even at these low levels of rent, something like 40 per cent of tenants take rent rebates.

The use of a rates subsidy to push rents even lower than historic costs adds further difficulty to the prediction of rent levels, for authorities use only their judgement in deciding how to split costs over rent and rates. Apart from making rent levels uncertain, the rate fund contribution is also questionable on grounds of equity. It is a subsidy to be analysed alongside government subsidies, but one raised from the local population rather than the national. It is not clear what is the purpose of subsidisation: is it to stimulate the housing stock or is it a form of poverty relief? Either way, it is difficult to see any logic in the use of local taxation rather than national.

Although rent levels are the result of pooling historic costs, net of subsidies, pooling does not imply uniformity.

Individual rents vary according to housing characteristics. Decisions on relative rents are again taken administratively.

SUMMARY

Clearly the rented market is unusual. Demand responds in a typical manner to a typical set of factors, but this is not true of supply. It is not reasonable to apply the usual profit motive to landlords. Some private sector suppliers are motivated in the manner discussed by economists in the theory of the firm, but by no means all. Public sector suppliers are motivated by entirely different considerations. In both sectors rents are not freely determined by the market.

Bibliography

[1] M. J. Artis, E. Kiernan and J. D. Whitley, 'Effects of Building Society Behaviour on Housing Investment', in *Contemporary Issues in Economics*, eds M. Parkin and A. R. Nobay (Manchester University Press, 1975).

[2] M. J. Ball, 'Recent Empirical Work on the Determination of Relative House Prices', *Urban Studies*, vol. 10 (1973).

[3] F. Berry, *Housing, The Great British Failure* (London: Charles Knight, 1974).

[4] J. Black, 'New Systems for Mortgages', *Lloyds Bank Review*, no. 111 (1974).

[5] M. Bowley, *The British Building Industry* (Cambridge University Press, 1966).

[6] Building and Civil Engineering Economic Development Committee's Joint Working Party Studying Public Sector Purchasing, *Report — The Public Client and the Construction Industries* (London: H.M.S.O., 1975).

[7] Building Societies Association, *Facts and Figures* (London: B.S.A., qtrly).

[8] I. L. R. Byatt, A. G. Holmans and D. E. W. Laidler, 'Income and the Demand for Housing', in *Essays in Modern Economics*, eds M. Parkin and A. R. Nobay (London: Longman, 1973).

[9] Central Statistical Office, *General Household Survey* (London: H.M.S.O., 1972).

[10] Central Statistical Office, *Social Trends* (London: H.M.S.O., ann.).

[11] C. Clark and G. T. Jones, *The Demand for Housing* (London: Centre for Environmental Studies, U.W.P. 11, 1971).

71

[12] E. J. Cleary, *The Building Society Movement* (London: Elek, 1965).

[13] D. Collard, 'Exclusion by Estate Agents: An Analysis', *Applied Economics*, vol. 5 (1973).

[14] M. H. Cooper and D. C. Stafford, 'A Note on the Economic Implications of Fair Rents', *Social and Economic Administration*, vol. 9 (1975).

[15] J. Cubbins, 'Price, Quality and Selling Time in the Housing Market', *Applied Economics*, vol. 6 (1974).

[16] J. B. Cullingworth, *Housing and Local Government* (London: Allen and Unwin, 1966).

[17] B. R. Davidson, 'The Effects of Land Speculation on the Supply of Housing in England and Wales, *Urban Studies*, vol. 12 (1975).

[18] F. De Leeuw, 'The Demand for Housing, a Review of Cross-Section Evidence, *Review of Economics and Statistics*, vol. LIII (1971).

[19] Department of the Environment, *Housing and Construction Statistics* (London: H.M.S.O., qtrly).

[20] Department of the Environment, *Housing Land Availability in the South-East* (London: H.M.S.O., 1975).

[21] Department of the Environment, *Manual on Local Authority Housing Subsidies and Accounting* (London: H.M.S.O., 1975).

[22] Department of the Environment, *Private Contractors' Construction Census* (London: H.M.S.O., ann.).

[23] A. W. Evans, 'Suggestions for the Reform of Housing Finance', in *Papers from Urban Economics Conference 1973* (London: Centre for Environmental Studies, C.P. 9, 1974).

[24] A. W. Evans, *The Economics of Residential Location* (London: Macmillan, 1973).

[25] M. C. Fleming, 'Economic Aspects of New Methods of Building, with particular reference to the British Isles, the Continent and America', *Journal of the Statistical and Social Inquiry Society of Ireland*, vol. XXI (1964-5).

[26] J. Foster, 'The Redistributive Effects of the Composite Income Tax Arrangement', *Manchester School*, vol. 43 (1975).

[27] M. Frankena, 'Alternative Models of Rent Control', *Urban Studies*, vol. 12 (1975).

[28] D. Ghosh, *The Economics of Building Societies* (Farnborough: Saxon House, 1974).

[29] B. Goodall, *The Economics of Urban Areas* (Oxford: Pergamon, 1972) ch. 6.

[30] T. J. Gough, 'The Inflation in New Private House Prices', *Economics*, vol. 10, autumn (1974).

[31] T. J. Gough, 'The Incidence of Government Housing Subsidies', *Housing and Planning Review*, vol. 31 (1975).

[32] M. Gray and M. Parkin, 'Housing Finance — A Realistic Solution', *The Banker*, vol. 124 (1974).

[33] W. G. Grigsby, *Housing Markets and Public Policy* (University of Pennsylvania Press, 1971).

[34] S. Haltermann, 'Areas of Urban Deprivation in Great Britain, an Analysis of 1971 Census Data', *Social Trends*, no. 6 (1975).

[35] R. Harding, 'Building Societies under Pressure', *The Banker*, vol. 123 (1973).

[36] R. L. Harrington, 'Housing Supply and Demand', *National Westminster Bank Review* (May 1972).

[37] P. M. Hillebrandt, *Economic Theory and the Construction Industry* (London: Macmillan, 1974).

[38] M. Hoffman, 'What Form should Housing Subsidies Take?', *Journal of Housing*, vol. 31 (1974).

[39] P. Holm, 'A Disaggregated Housing Market Model', in *Economic Problems of Housing*, ed. A. A. Nevitt (London: Macmillan, 1967).

[40] A. E. Holmans, 'A Forecast of Effective Demand for Housing in Great Britain', *Social Trends*, no. 1 (1970).

[41] Housing Centre Trust, *Housing Finance Review* (London: H.C.T., 1975).

[42] Housing Management Committee of the Central Housing Advisory Committee (Cullingworth), *Council Housing Purposes, Procedures and Priorities* (London: H.M.S.O., 1969).

[43] J. F. Kain and J. M. Quigley, 'Measuring the Value of

Housing Quality', *Journal of the American Statistics Association,* vol. 65 (1970).

[44] R. M. Kirwen and M. Ball, *The Economics of an Urban Housing Market* (London: Centre for Environmental Studies, R.P. 15, 1975).

[45] T. H. Lee, 'Housing and Permanent Income', *Review of Economics and Statistics,* vol. 50 (1968).

[46] C. Legg and M. Brion, 'Rent Rebates and Allowances — Are they being Claimed?', *Municipal Journal* (6 Dec 1974).

[47] A. J. Merrett and A. Sykes, *Housing Finance and Development* (London: Longman, 1965).

[48] Midland Bank Review, 'Problems of House Purchase', *Midland Bank Review,* no. v (1974).

[49] K. M. Miller and C. J. Fillein, *Housing Associations — 3 Surveys* (Birmingham: Centre for Urban and Regional Studies, 1971).

[50] A. Murie, 'Estimating Housing Need, Technique or Mystique?', *Housing Review* (May—June 1976).

[51] A. Murie, A. Niner and C. Watson, *Housing Policy and the Housing System* (London: Allen and Unwin, 1976).

[52] R. F. Muth, 'The Demand for Non-Farm Housing', in *The Demand for Durable Goods,* ed. A. C. Harberger (University of Chicago Press, 1960).

[53] R. F. Muth, *Cities and Housing* (University of Chicago Press, 1969).

[54] N.A.L.G.O. Working Party, *Housing, the Way Ahead* (London: N.A.L.G.O., 1973).

[55] National Board for Prices and Incomes, *Report No. 22, The Rate of Interest on Building Society Mortgages,* Cmnd 3136 (London: H.M.S.O., 1966).

[56] National Building Agency, *Trends in Housing and Construction* (London: N.B.A., 1976).

[57] L. Needleman, *The Economics of Housing* (London: Staples Press, 1965).

[58] L. Needleman, 'Rebuilding or Renovation? A Reply (to Sigsworth and Wilkinson)', *Urban Studies,* vol 5 (1968).

[59] L. Needleman, 'The Comparative Economics of Improvement and New Building', *Urban Studies*, vol. 6 (1969).

[60] A. A. Nevitt, *Housing Taxation and Subsidy* (London: Nelson, 1966).

[61] A. A. Nevitt, *The Nature of Rent Control Legislation in the U.K.* (London: Centre for Environmental Studies, U.W.P. 8, 1970).

[62] P. Niner, *Local Authority Housing Policy and Practice* (Birmingham: Centre for Urban and Regional Studies, 1975).

[63] Organisation for Economic Co-operation and Development, *Housing Finance, Present Problems* (Paris: O.E.C.D., 1974).

[64] C. Parker, 'Challenging Times for the Building Societies', *The Banker*, vol. 125 (1975).

[65] K. R. Parkinson, 'N.H.B.C. Council Dwellings — An Exercise in Common Sense', *Housing Review* (Mar—Apr 1976).

[66] R. Pollock, 'Supply of Residential Construction, a Cross-Section Examination of Recent Housing Market Behaviour', *Land Economics* (Feb 1973).

[67] S. J. Price, *Building Societies, The Origins and History* (London: Franey, 1958).

[68] M. G. Reid, *Housing and Income* (University of Chicago Press, 1962).

[69] H. W. Richardson, J. Vipond and R. A. Furbey, 'Determinants of Urban House Prices', *Urban Studies*, vol. 11 (1974).

[70] Scottish Housing Advisory Committee, *Report — Allocating Council Houses* (London: H.M.S.O., 1967).

[71] Scottish Housing Advisory Committee (Report of the Sub-Committee), *Demand for Private Houses in Scotland* (London: H.M.S.O., 1972).

[72] E. Sharp, 'Housing in Britain — Successes, Failures and the Future', *The 1970 Bellman Memorial Lecture* (Abbey National Building Society, 1971).

[73] G. Shea, 'House Purchase, The Case for a Junior Mort-

gage Market', *National Westminster Bank Review* (Feb 1971).

[74] E. M. Sigsworth and R. K. Wilkinson, 'Rebuilding or Renovation?', *Urban Studies,* vol. 4 (1967).

[75] E. M. Sigsworth and R. K. Wilkinson, 'Rebuilding or Renovation? A rejoinder', *Urban Studies,* vol. 7 (1970).

[76] E. M. Sigsworth and R. K. Wilkinson, 'Constraints on the Uptake of Improvement Grants', *Policy and Politics,* vol. 1 (Dec 1972).

[77] B. A. Smith 'The Supply of Urban Housing', *Quarterly Journal of Economics,* vol. xc (Aug 1976).

[78] D. C. Stafford, 'The Final Demise of the Private Landlord?, *Social and Economic Administration,* vol. 10 (1976).

[79] E. St J. O'Herlichy and J. E. Spencer, 'Building Society Behaviour 1955-70, *National Institute Economic Review,* no. 61 (Aug 1972).

[80] P. A. Stone, *Building Economy* (Oxford: Pergamon Press, 1966).

[81] P. A. Stone, *Urban Development in Britain: Standards, Costs and Resources,* vol. 1, Population Trends and Housing (Cambridge University Press, 1970).

[82] M. J. Vipond, 'Fluctuations in Private Housebuilding in Great Britain 1950-66', *Scottish Journal of Political Economy,* vol. 16 (1969).

[83] J. Vipond and J. B. Waller, 'The Determinants of Housing Expenditure and Owner Occupation', *Bulletin of the Oxford Institute for Economics and Statistics,* vol. 34 (1972).

[84] C. M. E. Whitehead, *The U.K. Housing Market* (Farnborough: Saxon House, 1974).

[85] C. M. E. Whitehead, and J. C. Odling-Smee, 'Long-run Equilibrium in Urban Housing — A Note', *Urban Studies,* vol. 12 (1975).

[86] R. K. Wilkinson, 'The Income Elasticity of Demand for Housing', *Oxford Economic Papers,* vol. 25 (1973).

[87] R. K. Wilkinson 'The Determinants of Relative House Prices (A comment on Ball's article, followed by a reply from Ball)', *Urban Studies,* vol. 11 (1974).

[88] H. L. Wolman, *Housing and Housing Policy in the U.S. and U.K.* (Lexington, Mass.: Lexington, 1975).
[89] M. Wray, 'Building Society Mortgages and the Housing Market', *Westminster Bank Review* (Feb 1968).